An Invitation to the Contemplative Life

Thomas Merton

Edited by Wayne Simsic

theWORD among us® press

The Word Among Us Press
9639 Doctor Perry Road
Ijamsville, Maryland 21754
www.wordamongus.org

ISBN 978-1-59325-085-0

11 10 09 08 07   2 3 4 5 6

Cover Design: DesignWorks Group
Book Design: David Crosson

Cover Image: Our Lady of Gethsemani Monastery © Harry Hinkle

Made and printed in the United States of America.

Library of Congress Cataloging-in-Publication Data

Merton, Thomas, 1915-1968.
  An invitation to the contemplative life / Thomas Merton; edited by
Wayne Simsic.
    p. cm.
  ISBN-13: 978-1-59325-085-0 (alk. paper)
  ISBN-10: 1-59325-085-1 (alk. paper)
  1. Contemplation. 2. Meditation. 3. Mysticism. 4. Prayer--Christianity. 5.
Spiritual life. 6. Christian life. I. Simsic, Wayne. II. Title.
  BV5091.C7M48 2006
  248.3'4--dc22
                                2006018009

Contents

Introduction

Thomas Merton, a twentieth-century Trappist monk, wrote passionately about spirituality and mysticism in a way that speaks to the hearts of women and men today. His outpouring of books explored the Desert Fathers, Christian mysticism, modern psychology, Eastern religions, literature, existentialism, and social issues. Not only do his writings uniquely blend monastic tradition and contemporary concerns, but they also map a modern contemplative's journey into the unknown in a quest for God. Though he never wanted a following, Thomas Merton has become one of the most beloved and influential spiritual masters of our time.

Merton's gift to all of us is this simple message: the contemplative experience, which uncovers our unity with the divine and a new vision of life, is not only for monks but for all Christians. He remarked, "Every man, to live a life full of significance, is called simply to know the significant interior of life" (*Honorable Reader: Reflections on My Work*, 39). Many feel that this Trappist monk addresses their deepest need for freedom based not on social approval but on direct dependence on an invisible God.

Loss and insecurity were strong threads in Merton's youth. He was born in France on January 31, 1915. His parents, Owen and Ruth, had met while studying in Paris under the same English painter, fallen in love, married, and moved to the south of France, where they could live simply and dedicate themselves to painting. But in the turmoil of the First World War, the family moved to Long Island, where John Paul, Thomas' only sibling, was born.

This journey would mark the beginning of many moves that loosened the ties Tom had to a geographical and emotional center. Even more dramatic were the death of his mother when he was only six and the death of his father when he was almost sixteen. These tragedies set the boy adrift on a pilgrimage that would continue for the rest of his life. His grandparents, Sam and Martha Jenkins, stabilized his life and showed him love and affection, but the time spent in boarding schools and the continual changes of address took their toll on him.

After his father's death, Tom spent school holidays with Tom Bennet, his father's doctor and wealthy friend. When he had the chance, he wandered around Europe alone, searching to find answers to his emotional hunger and to discover some antidote to his painful inner emptiness. During one of these trips he developed blood poisoning and, in the midst of overwhelming depression and a profound sense of aimlessness, was forced to face the depths of his apathy. A solution seemed to present itself in 1932 when he won a scholarship to Clare College, Cambridge. He entertained dreams of fine apparel, dating, conversing with intellectuals, writing, singing, and playing squash and tennis. Just before entering the college, however, around the time of his eighteenth birthday, Tom used the gift of tickets and money from Bennet to travel across France and to Rome. During his wanderings through early Christian churches and basilicas, he became fascinated by the beautiful Byzantine mosaics. It dawned on him that he had become a pilgrim and that the Byzantine crucifixes were speaking to him of something he was searching for. He prayed and read from a newly purchased Bible and, in his small room one night, received a vision of his father. His father's presence filled the room and, in a flash, uncovered the darkness in the soul of the young traveler: "I was filled with horror at what I saw and my whole being rose up in revolt against what was within me" (*The Seven Storey Mountain*, 111). As a young monk looking back on the experience in his autobiography, Thomas Merton lamented his lack of response to this extraordinary graced awareness.

Merton struggled at Clare College. He had a goal of joining the British diplomatic corps but sabotaged it by cutting classes, studying subjects he chose rather than the ones required, and losing himself in a party lifestyle. He fathered a child and was sent packing to the United States by his profoundly disappointed guardian, Tom Bennet. On the voyage back to his mother's parents in New York, Tom was overwhelmed with feelings of shame, guilt for betraying his father's expectations, and a sense of worthlessness.

After entering Columbia University, Tom experienced a minor breakdown and then slowly redirected his life. Though he was still unconsciously driven to find a way to fill the frightening abyss at the center of his being, for the first time he found intelligent, concerned friends who would support him—Bob Lax; Ed Rice; Sy Freedgood; literature professor Mark Van Doren, who inspired him to search for truth; and philosopher Daniel Walsh, who became a spiritual confidant and eventually joined the priesthood himself. Looking back on these relationships, Merton realized that they had saved him from inner chaos and given him necessary support to continue his journey. He also realized the strong influence of authors such as William Blake, Dante, and Jacques Maritain, as well as a variety of material— books, stories, music, ideas, poems, places, philosophies—that had become instruments of grace. It was hard for him to dismiss the fact that his entire life had been pulled toward God. Though at times he resisted the stirrings, he eventually responded to his heart's deep desire for conversion. On November 16, 1938, several friends from Columbia witnessed Thomas Merton's baptism into the Catholic faith at Corpus Christi Church. After years of searching and inner turmoil, Merton had made a decision to allow Christ to fill his emptiness with peace and a new reality.

Once he received his master's degree in literature in 1939, he made plans to study for a doctorate. However, his new religious belief had changed his vision, and he experienced a deep sense of peace and happiness. In the midst of this consolation, one question haunted him: Should he become a priest? Eventually he took a position in the English department at St. Bonaventure College and followed a strict regimen of prayer, liturgical worship, spiritual reading, and solitary walks. A retreat at the Abbey of Our Lady of Gethsemani in Kentucky only intensified Merton's longings for God. Eventually he realized that his heart was leading him to Gethsemani to become a Trappist monk. When he boarded the train on December 9, 1941, he saw that he was finally free—free because he now belonged completely to God.

At the time Merton joined the Trappists, formally known as the Cistercian Order of the Strict Observance, the community followed an austere regimen. The monks were dedicated to silence and contemplation, communicating only through sign language. Their food, clothing, and religious practices were medieval in origin. The life Merton encountered was one of simplicity, routine, silence, confinement, hard work, and prayer in community with over a hundred monks. Yet Merton responded with joyful enthusiasm; for the first time in his life, the pilgrim felt genuinely at home. He would later recall the time in the novitiate as physically hard but a happy time nevertheless.

Thomas Merton found peace in the new ordering of his life, the deep silence and solitude, and the physical beauty of the countryside. However, he discovered that outward changes did not damp the fires of his active intellect or curb his need to express a fertile imagination. He felt the urge to write, but he agonized over the suitability of writing in the life of a contemplative monk. Merton the writer continued to dream of possible books, while Merton the contemplative wanted to forsake writing and not look back. Merton the monk turned the dilemma over to his superiors. They told him to write, and he began by writing poems and short books on Cistercian life. Then in 1946 he began his autobiography, *The Seven Storey Mountain*.

In a private journal (eventually published as *The Sign of Jonas*), Merton referred to himself as "Jonas," identifying with the prophet who struggled with conflicting desires. As the time for his final vows approached, he not only struggled with being a writer in a monastery but also wondered whether the Trappists' monastic life was too active for him. Would he be happier in an order like the Carthusians that had fewer hours of work and public prayer, and more opportunity for solitude and private prayer? In 1948 Abbot James Fox, aware of Merton's need for solitude, allowed him to spend part of each Sunday in the woods. Later, as the monastery's new farm equipment increased the noise level, he offered Merton a vault and eventually a tool shed in the woods, which the young monk named St. Anne's Hermitage. It was a temporary solution, because Merton continued to explore the possibility of even greater solitude.

The publication of *The Seven Storey Mountain* in 1948 and its enormous popularity changed Merton's life and heightened the tension between writing and contemplative living. Reflecting the theological outlook of 1940s Catholicism and Merton's youthful idealism, the book became a national best seller and has remained in print ever since. Its success brought international attention to the Trappist monastery isolated in rural Kentucky. Suddenly men besieged Gethsemani wanting to become Trappists, and people of all ages sent fan mail. Merton began to accept himself as a Trappist monk who was also a writer.

However, shortly before his ordination, doubts began to return. The young monk felt paralyzed, unable to pray or to write. The day before he was ordained his journal entry described a life that seemed ready to crash, pulled down by confusion and despair. Yet he persevered in the darkness and discovered renewed peace. Thomas Merton became Father Louis on May 26, 1949.

In 1951, Merton was appointed master of scholastics, which meant that he would direct the spiritual growth and study of young professed monks. He was a gifted teacher, and his students appreciated his wisdom and loving care. Even though this new responsibility limited his time, he continued his writing. His appreciation of the contemplative path grew to include responsibility and compassion for people.

On March 18, 1958, Merton was in Louisville on an errand related to the printing of the postulants' guide, when, in a flash of intuition, he became aware of his connection with all people: "In Louisville, at the corner of Fourth and Walnut, in the center of the shopping district, I was suddenly overwhelmed with the realization that I loved all those people" (*Conjectures of a Guilty Bystander*, 156). He came to realize that holiness did not require isolation and renunciation of the world but was deeply inter-twined with the lives of other human beings. Merton's contempt for the "world" outside the monastery gave way to a need for solidarity with the disenfranchised. Though still actively engaged in the life of the monastery, he turned more attention to matters of justice and peace. In one of his books, he described himself as a "guilty bystander" in a turbulent, desperate, cynical, and violent world. Unable to march, Merton ministered to the world through his continued writing and through his influence on activists and others who visited him. He taught that the desire for peace is rooted in the spiritual life, and that without the contemplative or inner dimension, any action would go awry. As a young man, he had taken refuge from the world in order to find union with God. Now he realized that the intense struggle for this union called him to engage the world and to work for peace and equal-ity among his brothers and sisters. He wrote, "The monastery is not an escape from the world. On the contrary, by being in the monastery I take my true part in all the struggles and sufferings of the world" (*Honorable Reader*, 65).

In August 1965 Abbot Dom James gave Merton permission to live as a full-time hermit in a cinder-block cottage set on a knoll not quite a mile from the abbey. Between letter writing and visi-tors—scholars, peace activists, writers, theologians, and friends—his solitude was not ideal, but he settled in and immersed himself in a hermit-like existence. On an ordinary day, he prayed, swept, cleaned, cut wood, and wrote. He celebrated the Eucharist at the monastery but took his meals at the hermitage. His life was made difficult by dermatitis, surgery for bursitis, and allergies. When he discovered that the stream from which he had been draw-ing water was polluted, he had to carry water to the hermitage.

Despite the ruggedness of his lifestyle, Merton cherished the time to walk in the woods before daybreak, the company of creatures, and the hours of uninterrupted prayer.

When Flavian Burns became abbot, he gave Merton permission to travel to the East for a conference on monasticism and East-West dialogue. Merton had a long-standing interest in other Christian communities and in other religions. Eastern religions, especially Zen Buddhism, intrigued him. Though Merton realized that the exchange had limitations due to doctrinal differences, he thrived on interreligious dialogue and believed that Christians are called to unity with all humankind. He saw himself as a wisdom seeker, not as a renowned figure. In India he met the Dalai Lama and other holy men. People, whether cab drivers, monks, or nuns, immediately responded to his intellect, his charm, and his spirituality. In Sri Lanka he was deeply moved by seeing a colossal Buddha figure carved out of rock and experienced an extraordinary sense of inner clarity.

On December 10, 1968, Merton gave his final talk at a Bangkok conference. His thesis: inner transformation is at the heart of the monastic vow. At about 4:00 p.m., during the recess following Merton's presentation, a priest went to check on him and found the monk dead, apparently electrocuted by a defective fan. The icon Merton had with him when he died contained these words: "If we wish to please the true God and to be friends with the most blessed of friendships, let us present our spirit naked to God." Merton's body was flown back to the United States in the company of Americans killed in the Vietnam War, the very war he had protested.

After a funeral Mass at Gethsemani attended by lay and religious friends, his brother monks buried Merton in a small cemetery next to the abbey church. At the end of the service, the following words were read from the conclusion of *The Seven Storey Mountain*: "But you shall taste the true solitude of my anguish and my poverty and I shall lead you into the high places of my joy and you shall die in Me and find all things in My mercy" (422).

Since his death there has been a general consensus that Thomas Merton is a spiritual master for our times. He offers us a vast wealth of knowledge, wisdom, and spiritual nourishment from his pilgrimage and contemplative experience as a Trappist monk. His writings invite us to turn inward and explore our own depths, and in doing so, to become sensitive to the depths of the universal human spirit. Merton believed that we cannot have access to the heart of the world unless we first know our own truth. This is a spiritual path that we can all embrace. The chapters that follow highlight the main themes of Merton's contemplative journey. Each begins with a short introduction outlining the theme, followed by pertinent passages from Merton's writings. Passing over into his spirit and identifying with it, we can uncover our own unique path inward and realize that we too can receive the gift of the contemplative experience.

PART 1

The Search for Freedom

From the beginning to the end of his autobiography *The Seven Storey Mountain*, Merton's search for freedom is the predominant theme. During his public-school and university years, Merton was enslaved to his desires and sought to live without restriction. He mistakenly considered this way of living to be true freedom. Not until the age of twenty-seven, when he entered the Trappist community and embraced monastic self-discipline and a contemplative calling, did he let go of his illusion of freedom, with its attachments, values, and comforts. At that point he was able to welcome a new freedom, the freedom to love.

For Merton, the search for freedom marks the beginning of any serious response to the contemplative life. He taught that lack of freedom is a universal condition from which we need to be delivered. Because of original sin we do not possess the innocence that would allow us to see reality as God sees it; as a result, we must contend with a multitude of illusions that hide the truth, distort our vision, and enslave us. The primary question is not "How can I be happy?" but rather "How can I be free?"

The return to freedom requires sacrifice and the ability to say no. Essentially we have to renounce the illusion of freedom that society offers for the sake of true freedom, the freedom of our relationship with God. Freedom also requires that we say yes—yes to whatever God asks from us. We listen to the depths of our being and respond to God's call to become a new person. Through the healing power of Christ's resurrection, each person has been given the grace to become a new person in Christ—a whole person no longer dominated by external things but empowered by authentic freedom.

The selections in this chapter describe the desire for freedom and an awakening to the illusions and obsessions that hinder the growth of authentic liberty in God. Read together, they introduce what it means to reorient ourselves to the one true good, which is God. 🌿

I Will Trust You Always

My Lord God, I have no idea where I am going. I do not see the road ahead of me. I cannot know for certain where it will end. Nor do I really know myself, and the fact that I think I am following your will does not mean that I am actually doing so. But I believe that the desire to please you does in fact please you. And I hope I have that desire in all that I am doing. I hope that I will never do anything apart from that desire. And I know that if I do this you will lead me by the right road, though I may know nothing about it. Therefore I will trust you always though I may seem to be lost and in the shadow of death. I will not fear, for you are ever with me, and you will never leave me to face my perils alone.

Thoughts in Solitude

God's Love Warms Me

It is God's love that warms me in the sun and God's love that sends the cold rain. It is God's love that feeds me in the bread I eat and God that feeds me also by hunger and fasting. It is the love of God that sends the winter days when I am cold and sick, and the hot summer when I labor and my clothes are full of sweat: but it is God Who breathes on me with light winds off the river and in the breezes out of the wood. His love spreads the shade of the sycamore over my head and sends the water-boy along the edge of the wheat field with a bucket from the spring, while the laborers are resting and the mules stand under the tree.

It is God's love that speaks to me in the birds and streams; but also behind the clamor of the city God speaks to me in His judgments, and all these things are seeds sent to me from His will.

If these seeds would take root in my liberty, and if His will would grow from my freedom, I would become the love that He is, and my harvest would be His glory and my own joy.

New Seeds of Contemplation

Recognizing Our Poverty

The more we are content with our own poverty the closer we are to God, for then we accept our poverty in peace, expecting nothing from ourselves and everything from God.

Poverty is the door to freedom, not because we remain imprisoned in the anxiety and constraint which poverty of itself implies, but because, finding nothing in ourselves that is a source of hope, we know there is nothing in ourselves worth defending. There is nothing special in ourselves to love. We go out of ourselves therefore and rest in Him in Whom alone is our hope.

. . . What is the use of knowing our weakness if we do not implore God to sustain us with His power? What is the value of recognizing our poverty if we never use it to entreat his mercy? . . . The value of our weakness and of our poverty is that they are the earth in which God sows the seed of desire. And no matter how abandoned we may seem to be, the confident desire to love Him in spite of our abject misery is the sign of His presence and the pledge of our salvation.

Thoughts in Solitude

To Be Grateful

Our knowledge of God is perfected by gratitude: we are thankful and rejoice in the experience of the truth that He is love.

. . . Gratitude, though, is more than a mental exercise, more than a formula of words. We cannot be satisfied to make a mental note of things which God has done for us and then perfunctorily thank Him for favors received.

To be grateful is to recognize the Love of God in everything He has given us—and He has given us everything. Every breath we draw is a gift of His love, every moment of existence is a grace, for it brings with it immense graces from Him. Gratitude therefore takes nothing for granted, is never unresponsive, is constantly awakening to new wonder and to praise of the goodness of God. For the grateful man knows that God is good, not by hearsay but by experience. And that is what makes the difference.

Thoughts in Solitude

An Instinct for Renewal

Man in modern technological society has begun to be callous and disillusioned. He has learned to suspect what claims to be new, to doubt all the "latest" in everything. He is drawn instinctively to the new, and yet he sees in it nothing but the same old sham. The specious glitter of newness, the pretended creativity of a society in which youthfulness is commercialized and the young are old before they are twenty, fills some hearts with utter despair. There seems to be no way to find any real change. "The more things change," says a French proverb, "the more they are the same."

Yet in the deepest ground of our being we still hear the insistent voice which tells us: "You must be born again."

There is in us an instinct for newness, for renewal, for a liberation of creative power. We seek to awaken in ourselves a force which really changes our lives from within. And yet the same instinct tells us that this change is a recovery of that which is deepest, most original, most personal in ourselves. To be born again is not to become somebody else, *but to become ourselves.*

The deepest spiritual instinct in man is that urge of inner truth which demands that he be faithful to himself: to his deepest and most original potentialities. Yet at the same time, in order to become oneself, one must die. That is to say, in order to become one's true self, the false self must die. In order for the inner self to appear, the outer self must disappear: or at least become secondary, unimportant.

Love and Living

Birth in the Spirit

The rebirth of which Christ speaks is not a single event but a continuous dynamic of inner renewal. Certainly, sacramental baptism, the "birth by water," can be given only once. But birth in the Spirit happens many times in a man's life, as he passes through successive stages of spiritual development. A false and superficial view of Christianity assumes that it is enough to be baptized with water and to observe certain ethical and ritual prescriptions in order to guarantee for oneself a happy life in the other world. But this is only a naive view of Christianity. True Christianity is growth in the life of the Spirit, a deepening of the new life, a continuous rebirth, in which the exterior and superficial life of the ego-self is discarded like an old snake skin and the mysterious, invisible self of the Spirit becomes more present and more active. The true Christian rebirth is a renewed transformation, a "passover" in which man is progressively liberated from selfishness and not only grows in love but in some sense "becomes love." The perfection of the new birth is reached where there is no more selfishness, there is only love. In the language of the mystics, there is no more ego-self, there is only Christ; self no longer acts, only the Spirit acts in pure love. The perfect illumination is, then, the illumination of Love shining by itself. To become completely transparent and allow Love to shine by itself is the maturity of the "New Man."

Love and Living

Developing Our Freedom

If God made us intelligent and free, it was in order that we might develop our freedom, extend our powers and capacities of willing and loving to an unbelievable breadth, and raise our minds to an unheard of vision of truth. But in order that we might do all this (which is quite beyond our natural powers), He Himself adds to our natural gifts the gifts of grace which elevate and transfigure our nature, healing its ills and expanding its powers, bringing forth into actuality all its hidden resources in order to develop them yet more by our mystical life in God.

. . . The Holy Spirit comes to set the whole house of our soul in order, to deliver our minds from immaturity, alienation, fear, and tenacious prejudice. If Christ is the Lamb of God Who takes away sins of the world, then surely He sends His Spirit to deliver our souls from obsession with our feelings of guilt. This is the one thing so many Christians refuse to see. They think Christ's power to deliver us from sin is not a real liberation but an assertion of His own rights over us. The truth is that it is both, for when God asserts "His rights" over us we become free. God is Truth and "The truth shall make you free."

This is precisely what we fail to understand. With respect to the higher freedom of grace, our natural freedom is simply a potency waiting to be developed. It is paradoxically by the grace of God that we finally achieve our full spiritual freedom, and it is a gift of God that enables us to stand on our own feet.

The New Man

To Find the Meaning of Our Lives

To find the full meaning of our existence, we must find not the meaning that we expect but the meaning that is revealed to us by God. The meaning that comes to us out of the transcendent darkness of His mystery and our own. We do not know God and we do not know ourselves. How then can we imagine that it is possible for us to chart our own course toward the discovery of the meaning of our life? This meaning is not a sun that rises every morning, though we have come to think that it does, and on mornings when it does not rise we substitute some artificial light of our own so as not to admit that this morning was absurd.

Meaning is, then, not something we discover in ourselves, or in our lives. The meanings we are capable of discovering are never sufficient. The true meaning has to be revealed. It has to be "given." And the fact that it is given is, indeed, the greater part of its significance: for life itself is, in the end, only significant in so far as it is given.

As long as we experience life and existence as suns that have to rise every morning, we are in agony. We must learn that life is a light that rises when God summons it out of darkness. For this there are no fixed times.

The New Man

Free in the Love of God

In planning the course of our lives, we must remember the importance and the dignity of our own freedom. A man who fears to settle his future by a good act of his own free choice does not understand the love of God. For our freedom is a gift God has given us in order that He may be able to love us more perfectly, and be loved by us more perfectly in return.

Love is perfect in proportion to its freedom. It is free in proportion to its purity. We act most freely when we act purely in response to the love of God. But the purest love of God is not servile, not blind, not limited by fear. Pure charity is fully aware of the power of its own freedom. Perfectly confident of being loved by God, the soul that loves Him dares to make a choice of its own, knowing that its own choice will be acceptable to love.

. . . We know when we are following our vocation when our soul is set free from preoccupation with itself and is able to seek God and even to find Him, even though it may not appear to find Him. Gratitude and confidence and freedom from ourselves: these are signs that we have found our vocation and are living up to it even though everything else may seem to have gone wrong. They give us peace in any suffering. They teach us to laugh at despair. And we may have to.

There is something in the depths of our being that hungers for wholeness and finality. Because we are made for eternal life, we are made for an act that gathers up all the powers and capacities of our being and offers them simultaneously and forever to God. The blind spiritual instinct that tells us obscurely that our own lives have a particular importance and purpose, and which urges us to find out our vocation, seeks in so doing to bring us to a decision that will dedicate our lives irrevocably to their true purpose.

No Man Is an Island

The One Thing Necessary

One of the chief obstacles to this perfection of selfless charity is the selfish anxiety to get the most out of everything, to be a brilliant success in our own eyes and in the eyes of other men. We can only get rid of this anxiety by being content to miss something in almost everything we do. We cannot master everything, taste everything, understand everything, drain every experience to its last dregs. But if we have the courage to let almost everything else go, we will probably be able to retain the one thing necessary for us—whatever it may be. If we are too eager to have everything, we will almost certainly miss even the one thing we need.

Happiness consists in finding out precisely what the "one thing necessary" may be in our lives, and in gladly relinquishing all the rest. For then, by a divine paradox, we find that everything else is given us together with the one thing we needed.

No Man Is an Island

Concern with Temporal Things

My intention is to give myself entirely and without compromise to whatever work God wants to perform in me and through me. But this gift is not something absolutely blind and without definition. It is already defined by the fact that God has given me a *contemplative* vocation. By so doing He has signified a certain path, a certain goal to be mine. That is what I am to keep in view, because that is His will. It means renouncing the business, ambitions, honors and pleasures and other activities of the world. It means only a minimum of concern with temporal things.

The Sign of Jonas

Surrendering to the Will of God

All good, all perfection, all happiness, are found in the infinitely good and perfect and blessed will of God. Since true freedom means the ability to desire and choose, always, without error, without defection, what is really good, then freedom can only be found in perfect union and submission to the will of God. If our will travels with His, it will reach the same end, rest in the same peace, and be filled with the same infinite happiness that is His.

Therefore, the simplest definition of freedom is this: it means the ability to do the will of God. To be able to resist His will is not to be free. In sin there is no true freedom.

. . . Our true liberty is something we must never sacrifice, for if we sacrifice it we renounce God Himself. Only the false spontaneity of caprice, the pseudo liberty of sin, is to be sacrificed. Our true liberty must be defended with life itself for it's the most precious element in our being. It is our liberty that makes us Persons, constituted in the divine image.

New Seeds of Contemplation

To Be a Saint

For me to be a saint means to be myself. Therefore the problem of sanctity and salvation is in fact the problem of finding out who I am and of discovering my true self.

Trees and animals have no problem. God makes them what they are without consulting them, and they are satisfied.

With us it is different. God leaves us free to be whatever we like. We can be ourselves or not, as we please. We are at liberty to be real or to be unreal. We may be true or false, the choice is ours. We may wear now one mask and now another, and never, if we so desire, appear with our own true face. But we cannot make these choices with impunity. Causes have effects, and if we lie to ourselves and to others, then we cannot expect to find truth and reality whenever we happen to want them. If we have chosen the way of falsity, we must not be surprised that truth eludes us when we finally come to need it!

Our vocation is not simply to *be*, but to work together with God in the creation of our own life, our own identity, our own destiny. We are free beings and sons of God. This means to say that we should not passively exist, but actively participate in His creative freedom, in our own lives, and in the lives of others, by choosing the truth.

New Seeds of Contemplation

Liberation from Cultural Delusions

My conversion to the Christian faith, or to be precise my conversion to Christ, is something I have always regarded as a radical liberation from the delusions and obsessions of modern man and his society. I have always believed and continue to believe that faith is the only real protection against the absorption of freedom and intelligence in the crass and thoughtless servitude of mass society. Religious faith, and faith alone, can open the inner ground of man's being to the liberty of the sons of God, and preserve him from the surrender of his integrity to the seduction of a totalitarian life. The reason for this is that no matter what man thinks, his thought is based on a fundamental belief of some sort. If his belief is in slogans and doctrines which are foisted on him by a political or economic ideology, he will surrender his inmost truth to an exterior compulsion. If his belief is a suspension of belief, and an acceptance of physical stimulation for its own sake, he still continues to "believe" in the possibility of some rational happiness to be attained in this manner. Man must believe in something, and that in which he believes becomes his god. To serve some material or human entity as one's god is to be a slave of that which perishes, and thus to be a slave of death, sorrow, falsehood, misery. The only true liberty is in the service of that which is beyond all limits, beyond all definitions, beyond all human appreciation: that which is All, and which therefore is no limited or individual thing. . . .

Honorable Reader

Living in Full Awareness of God

I think that, like most other converts, I faced the problem of the "religiousness" and came to terms with it. God was not for me a working hypothesis, to fill in gaps left open by a scientific world view. Nor was He a God enthroned somewhere in outer space. Nor did I ever feel any particular "need" for superficial religious routines merely to keep myself happy. I would even say that, like most modern men, I have not been much moved by the concept of "getting into heaven" after muddling through this present life. On the contrary, my conversion to Catholicism began with the realization of the presence of God *in this present life*, in the world and in myself, and that my task as a Christian is to live in full and vital awareness of this ground of my being and of the world's being.

Conjectures of a Guilty Bystander

PART 2

The Contemplative Way

The contemplative path certainly does not require that everyone enter a religious community. But it always demands a reordering of our priorities, our sense of self, and our way of life. We choose a life grounded in a relationship with Christ that is nourished by prayer and meditation. The contemplative way for Merton is primarily an inner journey. We can easily ignore our spiritual lives by letting ourselves be pulled outward by any number of diversions. Many of us are so involved in a busy life that we have no time to focus inward. As a result, we lose our moorings, drift away from a spiritual center, and become overwhelmed and lost.

Moving inward also means relating to God within. However, Merton reminds us that God is beyond ideas and images, because these can only represent God in a limited way. We don't really know God and should accept that ultimately the divine will remain a mystery. Merton himself refers to this reality of God as "the Hidden Ground of Love." Only in relating to "the Hidden Ground of Love," he contends, can we find our authentic freedom and a new vision of the world; and only in communion with this unknown ground of love can we find communion with others.

This chapter describes the contemplative life as uncovering the God within who seeks us in every part of our lives. Remembering that God is not an object we control, we follow the Spirit wherever it blows, even into the wilderness, where we lose our comfortable and secure idea of both self and God.

God Seeks Us

God seeks Himself in us, and the aridity and sorrow of our heart is the sorrow of God who is not known to us, who cannot yet find Himself in us because we do not dare to believe or trust the incredible truth that He could live in us, and live there out of choice, out of preference. But indeed we exist solely for this, to be the place He has chosen for His presence, His manifestation in the world, His epiphany. But we make all this dark and inglorious because we fail to believe it, we refuse to believe it. It is not that we hate God, rather that we hate ourselves, despair of ourselves. If we once began to recognize, humbly but truly, the real value of our own self, we would see that this value was the sign of God in our being, the signature of God upon our being. Fortunately, the love of our fellow man is given us as the way of realizing this. For the love of our brother, our sister, our beloved, our wife, our child, is there to see with the clarity of God Himself that we are good. It is the love of my lover, my brother or my child that sees God in me, makes God credible to myself in me. And it is my love for my lover, my child, my brother, that enables me to show God to him or her in himself or herself. Love is the epiphany of God in our poverty. The contemplative life is then the search for peace not in an abstract exclusion of all outside reality, not in a barren negative closing of the senses upon the world, but in the openness of love.

The Monastic Journey

What Is the Contemplative Life?

What do we think the contemplative life is? How do we conceive it? As a life of withdrawal, tranquility, retirement, silence? Do we keep ourselves apart from action and change in order to learn techniques for entering into a kind of static present reality which is there and which we have to learn how to penetrate? Is contemplation an objective static "thing," like a building, for which there is a key? Do you hunt for this key, find it, then unlock the door and enter? Well, that is a valid image from a certain point of view, but it isn't the only image.

The contemplative life isn't something objective that is "there" and to which, after fumbling around, you finally gain access. The contemplative life is a dimension of our subjective existence. Discovering the contemplative life is a new self-discovery. One might say it is the flowering of a deeper identity on an entirely different plane from a mere psychological discovery, a paradoxical new identity that is found only in loss of self. To find one's self by losing one's self: that is part of "contemplation." Remember the Gospel, "He who would save his life must lose it."

The contemplative experience originates from this totally new kind of awareness of the fact that we are most truly ourselves when we lose ourselves. We become ourselves when we find ourselves in Christ.

. . . Nor is anyone asserting that contemplatives in this sense are found only in cloisters. . . . There are plenty of housewives with noisy children and all kinds of duties who are leading a contemplative life in this sense. And there are plenty of people teaching in universities or engaged in intellectual life in one form or other who are or can be contemplatives in this sense without very much difficulty.

Contemplation in a World of Action

Knowing the Presence of God

The heart of the Christian mystical experience is that it experiences the ineffable reality of what is beyond experience. It "knows" the presence of God, not in clear vision but "as unknown" (*tanquam ignotum*). Christian faith too, while of course concerning itself with certain truths that have been revealed by God, does not terminate in the conceptual formulation of those truths. It goes beyond words and ideas and attains to God himself. But the God who in a certain sense is "known" in the articles of faith is "known as unknown" beyond those articles. One might even say, with some of the Fathers of the Church, that while our concepts may tell us that "God is," our knowledge of God beyond those concepts is a knowledge of Him "as though He were not" since His Being is not accessible to us in direct experience. We are persuaded that many who consider themselves atheists are in fact persons who are discontented with a naive idea of God which makes Him appear to be an "object" or a "thing," or a person in a merely finite and human sense. . . .

Now, while the Christian contemplative must certainly develop, by study, the theological understanding of concepts about God, he is called mainly to penetrate the wordless darkness and apophatic light of an experience beyond concepts. . . .

. . . What is called the contemplative life is really a life arranged in such a way that a person can more easily and more simply and more naturally live in an awareness of direct dependence on God—almost with the sense of realizing consciously, at every moment, how much we depend on Him; and receive from Him directly everything that comes to us as a pure gift; and experience, taste in our hearts, the love of God in this gift, the delicacy and the personal attention of God to us in His merciful love. . . .

Contemplation in a World of Action

God Dwells Within

The Christian is then not simply a man of good will, who commits himself to a certain set of beliefs, who has a definite dogmatic conception of the universe, of man, and of man's reason for existing. He is not simply one who follows a moral code of brotherhood and benevolence with strong emphasis on certain rewards and punishments dealt out to the individual. Underlying Christianity is not simply a set of doctrines about God considered as dwelling remotely in heaven, and man struggling on earth, far from heaven, trying to appease a distant God by means of virtuous acts. On the contrary, Christians themselves too often fail to realize that the infinite God is dwelling within them, so that He is in them and they are in Him. They remain unaware of the presence of the infinite source of being right in the midst of the world and of men. True Christian wisdom is therefore oriented to the experience of divine Light which is present in the world, the Light in whom all things are, and which is nevertheless unknown to the world because no mind can see or grasp its infinity.

Contemplative wisdom is then . . . a living contact with the Infinite Source of all being, a contact not only of minds and hearts, not only of "I and Thou," but a transcendent union of consciousness in which man and God become, according to the expression of St. Paul, "one spirit."

Honorable Reader

My Life as Gift

It seems to me that one of the most basic experiences of anyone who gets down into any kind of depth is the breakthrough realization that *I am*. This is quite normal for any youngster of eight or nine. There's a point in your life where maybe you're just playing around and all of a sudden it hits you between the eyes that *you* really *are*. This is a true grasp of what being is. It isn't that you understand a definition of being. You are simply overwhelmed by the *fact* of being. This is the place where God's reality is going to break through. I become aware of my own reality, and then God's reality turns out to be the ground of mine.

. . . But this basic sense of our own being can be blocked, maybe by a refusal to take things in terms of gift, or by our not wanting to have to say thanks to anybody. Or maybe we want to have life on our own terms, as if it were not a gift but *my due*. This attitude goes back to a legalism which is terrible, precisely because, instead of making it possible to accept life as a gift, welling up from within, I make it something that's coming to me, something I'm owed.

The Springs of Contemplation

Where Are You?

There is something left in the depths of our being which is this yes to God. . . . It is something we experience as basic to our being. If we reflect and think, we sense that the whole meaning of our life consists in this yes to God. Something in us wants to say this yes. By it, we acknowledge that God is all, and that from God, whom we praise and love and glorify, we receive everything. All life flows out of this deep yes to God.

One of the new commentators on Genesis has God coming to Adam after the Fall and asking, "Adam, where are you?" Early Church writers have similar passages which are very beautiful. We also live this. We experience in the contemplative life a manifestation of God, who asks us, "Where are you?" and we realize we're not around. In other words, this question is a way of God reminding us that we are not where we ought to be, which is right in God. This recurs all through our life. God keeps calling us back with words like these.

The Springs of Contemplation

God Finds Himself in Us

God knows us from within ourselves, not as objects, not as strangers, not as intimates, but as our own selves. His knowledge of us is the pure light of which our own self-knowledge is only a dim reflection. He knows us in Himself, not merely as images of something outside Him, but as "selves" in which His own self is expressed. He finds Himself more perfectly in us than we find ourselves.

No Man Is an Island

Following the Spirit

Whoever seeks to catch Him and hold Him loses Him. He is like the wind that blows where it pleases. You who love Him must love Him as arriving from where you do not know and as going where you do not know. Your spirit must seek to be as clean and as free as His own Spirit, in order to follow Him wherever He goes. Who are we to call ourselves either clean or free, unless He makes us so?

If He should teach us how to follow Him into the wilderness of His own freedom, we will no longer know where we are, because we are with Him Who is everywhere and nowhere at the same time.

Those who love only His apparent presence cannot follow the Lord wherever He goes. They do not love Him perfectly if they do not allow Him to be absent. They do not respect His liberty to do as He pleases. They think their prayers have made them able to command Him, and to subject His will to their own.

No Man Is an Island

God Is Not an Object

God is not an object. God is not one thing among other things, and if you set God up in contrast to everything else, you are going to have insuperable trouble. If I have to maintain the idea of God against the idea of everything else, I am going to have to fight everything in the universe because sooner or later some other idea is going to pop up. But the idea of God is not God Himself, and God is not opposed to anything; God is not opposed to any of His creatures.

. . . You have to take God and creatures all together and see God in His creation and creation in God and don't ever separate them. Then everything manifests God instead of hiding God or being in the way of God as obstacle.

Thomas Merton in Alaska

To Be a Good Catholic

The discipline of the contemplative in the world is first of all the discipline of fidelity to his duty of state—to his obligations as head of a family, as a member of a profession, as a citizen. This discipline, these duties can demand very great sacrifices. Perhaps, indeed, some of the difficulties of people in the world exact of them far greater sacrifice than they would find in the cloister. In any case, their contemplative life will be deepened and elevated by the depth of their understanding and their duties. . . . It is not sufficient to "be a good Catholic." One must penetrate the inner meaning of his life in Christ and see the full significance of its demands. One must carry out his obligations not as a question of form, but with a real, personal decision to offer the good he does to God, in and through Christ. . . .

It follows from this that for the married Christian, his married life is essentially bound up with his contemplation. This is inevitable. It is by his marriage that he is situated in the mystery of Christ. It is by his marriage that he bears witness to Christ's love for the world, and in his marriage that he experiences that love. His marriage is a sacramental center from which grace radiates out into every department of his life, and consequently it is his marriage that will enable his work, leisure, his sacrifices, and even his distractions to become in some degree contemplative. For by his marriage all these things are ordered to Christ and centered in Christ. It should above all be emphasized that for the married Christian, even and especially married love enters into his contemplation, and this, as a matter of fact, gives it a special character.

The Inner Experience

PART 3

Turning Back to the True Self

Looking back on his dissolute youth while writing *The Seven Storey Mountain*, Merton was mortified by a sense of self that was false, selfish, and empty. As a young monk, he realized that his recentering on God would be neither quick nor easy, and this knowledge troubled his soul. The gap between his own private idolatry and God's saving love was so wide that he became overwhelmed by fear.

Returning to God and our true self, Merton realized, means surrendering the false or shadow self. We need to affirm and love ourselves, but the "self" we need to affirm and love is often hidden beneath a mask. Although our real self is made in the image and likeness of God, too often the self we cultivate is only a disguise or a distortion of our true being. This false or illusory self is the one that thinks it can ultimately control its own fate. It tries to fill its emptiness with material possessions, food, drink, sex, or frenetic activity, but it is never satisfied. It does not believe in its own worth, so it is easily manipulated by the opinions and expectations of others. And it often succumbs to jealousy, because it perceives others as more beautiful, talented, or intelligent. This shadow self creates a world apart from God and becomes trapped by its own fantasy. It lives a lie because it refuses to recognize its vulnerability without God.

The true self lets go of any pretense to ultimate control. It embraces gifts, talents, skills, and body as wondrous graces from a loving God. The true self, mysterious and illusive because it is the self in God, seeks only to do the will of God, which is, simply put, to love. The true self finds rest in God's embrace; it is the self at home in the person of Jesus Christ. The false self, however, does not easily give way to the true self. Change is only possible with the grace that God gives freely to the humble heart that acknowledges its dependency. Even the urgency that nudges us to reclaim our life in God is a gift.

The selections that follow further describe the choice between our shadow or false self and our true self. They also highlight the conversion that occurs when we look for our identity hidden in the love and mercy of God. 🌿

We Have a Choice of Two Identities

Every one of us is shadowed by an illusory person: a false self.

This is the man that I want myself to be but who cannot exist, because God does not know anything about him. And to be unknown of God is altogether too much privacy.

My false and private self is the one who wants to exist outside the reach of God's will and God's love—outside of reality and outside of life. And such a self cannot help but be an illusion.

We are not very good at recognizing illusions, least of all the ones we cherish about ourselves—the ones we are born with and which feed the roots of sin. For most of the people in the world, there is no greater subjective reality than this false self of theirs, which cannot exist. A life devoted to the cult of this shadow is what is called a life of sin.

All sin starts from the assumption that my false self, the self that exists only in my own egocentric desires, is the fundamental reality of life to which everything else in the universe is ordered. Thus I use up my life in the desire for pleasures and the thirst for experiences, for power, honor, knowledge and love, to clothe this false self and construct its nothingness into something objectively real. . . .

The secret of my identity is hidden in the love and mercy of God.

But whatever is in God is really identical with Him, for His infinite simplicity admits no division and no distinction. Therefore I cannot hope to find myself anywhere except in Him.

. . . We have the choice of two identities: the external mask which seems to be real and which lives by a shadowy autonomy for the brief moment of earthly existence, and the hidden, inner person who seems to us to be nothing, but who can give himself eternally to the truth in whom he subsists. It is this inner self that is taken up into the mystery of Christ, by His love, by the Holy Spirit, so that in secret we live "in Christ."

Yet we must not deal in too negative a fashion even with the "external self." This self is not by nature evil, and the fact that it is unsubstantial is not to be imputed to it as some kind of crime. It is afflicted with metaphysical poverty: but all that is poor deserves mercy. So too our outward self: as long as it does not isolate itself in a lie, it is blessed by the mercy and the love of Christ.

New Seeds of Contemplation

The First Step to Wisdom

The first step in all this is to recognize our true condition. Before we can ever hope to find ourselves in God, we must clearly recognize the fact that we are far from Him. Before we can realize who we really are, we must become conscious of the fact that the person we think we are, here and now, is at best an impostor and a stranger. We must constantly question his motives and penetrate his disguises. Otherwise our attempts at self knowledge are bound to fail, for if we fully and complacently acquiesce in our illusion of who we are, our "self-knowledge" will only strive to reinforce our identification of ourselves with this impostor.

The New Man

The Spirit Undergoes a Conversion

It is quite usual, when a man comes into intimate spiritual contact with God, that he should feel himself entirely changed from within. Our spirit undergoes a conversion, a *metanoia,* which re-orientates our whole being after raising it to a new level, and even seems to change our whole nature itself. And then, "self-realization" becomes an awareness that we are quite different from our normal empirical selves. At the same time we are vividly conscious of the fact that this new mode of being is truly more "normal" than our own ordinary existence. It is more "natural" for us to be "out of ourselves" and carried freely and entirely towards the "Other"—towards God in Himself or in other men—than it is for us to be centered and enclosed in ourselves. We find ourselves to be most truly human when we are raised to the level of the divine.

. . . When the light of God's truth begins to find its way through the mists of illusion and self-deception with which we have unconsciously surrounded ourselves, and when the image of God within us begins to return to itself, the false self which we inherited from Adam begins to experience the strange panic that Adam felt when, after his sin, he hid in the trees of the garden because he heard the voice of the Lord God in the afternoon.

If we are to recover our own identity, and return to God by the way Adam came in his fall, we must learn to stop saying: "I heard you in the garden, and I was afraid, because I was naked. And I hid." (Genesis 2:10) We must cast away the "aprons of leaves" and the "garments of skins" which the Fathers of the Church variously interpret as passions, and attachments to earthly things, and fixation in our own rigid determination to be someone other than our true selves.

The New Man

To Be Aware of God

Self-realization in this true religious sense is then less an awareness of ourselves than an awareness of the God to whom we are drawn in the depths of our own being. We become real, and experience our actuality, not when we pause to reflect upon our own self as an isolated individual entity, but rather when, transcending ourselves and passing beyond reflection, we center our whole soul upon the God Who is our life. That is to say we fully "realize" ourselves when we cease to be conscious of ourselves in separateness and know nothing but the one God Who is above all knowledge.

We fully realize ourselves when all our awareness is of another—of Him Who is utterly "Other" than all beings because He is infinitely above them. The image of God is brought to life in us when it breaks free from the shroud and the tomb in which our self-consciousness had kept it prisoner, and loses itself in the total consciousness of Him Who is Holy. This is one of the main ways in which "he that would save his life will lose it" (Luke 9:24).

What this means in practice is fidelity and attentiveness to the Words of God. . . .To be "aware" of God is to enter into contact with One, Who, infinitely hidden and transcendent, cannot be known as He is in Himself unless He reveals Himself to us. But God speaks to us, in His Scriptures, and has given Himself to us in His Son—our whole life of faith is a life of attentiveness, of "listening" in order to receive the word of God into our hearts.

The New Man

The Pure Glory of God Within

At the center of our being is a point of nothingness which is untouched by sin and by illusion, a point of pure truth, a point or spark which belongs entirely to God, which is never at our disposal, from which God disposes of our lives, which is inaccessible to the fantasies of our own mind or the brutalities of our own will. This little point of nothingness and of *absolute poverty* is the pure glory of God in us. It is, so to speak, His name written in us, as our poverty, as our indigence, as our dependence, as our sonship. It is like a pure diamond, blazing with the invisible light of heaven. It is in everybody, and if we could see it we would see these billions of points of light coming together in the face and the blaze of a sun that would make all the darkness and cruelty of life vanish completely. . . . I have no program for this seeing. It is only given. But the gate of heaven is everywhere.

Conjectures of a Guilty Bystander

Seeking the Approval of Others

The man who is dominated by what I have called the "social image" is one who allows himself to see and to approve in himself only that which his society prescribes as beneficial and praiseworthy in its members. As a corollary he sees and disapproves (usually in *others*) mostly what his society disapproves. And yet he congratulates himself on "thinking for himself." In reality, this is only a game that he plays in his own mind—the game of substituting the words, slogans, and concepts he has received from society for genuine experiences of his own.

Disputed Questions

Nurturing the Seeds of Divine Life

The seeds of this sublime life are planted in every Christian soul at Baptism. But seeds must grow and develop before you reap the harvest. There are thousands of Christians walking about the face of the earth bearing in their bodies the infinite God of Whom they know practically nothing. They are themselves sons of God and are not aware of their identity. Instead of seeking to know themselves and their true dignity, they struggle miserably to impersonate the alienated characters whose "greatness" rests on violence, craftiness, lust, and greed.

The seeds of contemplation and sanctity, planted in those souls, merely lie dormant. They do not germinate. They do not grow. In other words, sanctifying grace occupies the substance of their souls, but never flows out to inflame and irrigate and take possession of their faculties, their intellect and will. The presence of God never becomes an intimate reality. God does not manifest Himself to these souls because they do not seek Him with any real desire.

They are men divided between God and the world. They are at home only in their exterior self. They never seek what is deeper within them. They allow God to maintain His rights over the substance of their souls, but their thoughts and desires do not belong to Him. They belong to illusion, to passion, and to external things. Consequently, as far as their knowledge of God is concerned, these Christians are in the same condition as men without God.

The Inner Experience

The Inner Self

The inner self is precisely that self which cannot be tricked or manipulated by anyone, even by the devil. He is like a very shy wild animal that never appears at all whenever an alien presence is at hand, and comes out only when all is perfectly *peaceful*, in silence, when he is untroubled and alone. He cannot be lured by anyone or anything, because he responds to no lure except that of the divine freedom.

Sad is the case of that exterior self that imagines himself contemplative, and seeks to achieve contemplation as the fruit of planned effort and of spiritual ambition. He will assume varied attitudes, meditate on the inner significance of his own postures, and try to fabricate for himself a contemplative identity: and all the while there is nobody there. There is only an illusory, fictional "I" which seeks itself, struggles to create itself out of nothing, maintained in being by its own compulsion and the prisoner of his private illusion.

The call to contemplation is not, and cannot, be addressed to such an "I."

The Inner Experience

Our Substantial Reality

The inner self is not a part of our being, like a motor in a car. It is our entire substantial reality itself, on its highest and most personal and most existential level. It is like life, and it is life: it is our spiritual life when it is most alive. It is the life by which everything else in us lives and moves. It is in and through and beyond everything that we are. If it is awakened, it communicates a new life to the intelligence in which it lives, so that it becomes a living awareness of itself: and this awareness is not so much something that we ourselves have, as something that we are.

The inner self is as secret as God and, like Him, it evades every concept that tries to seize hold of it with full possession. It is a life that cannot be held and studied as object, because it is not "a thing." It is not reached and coaxed forth from hiding by any process under the sun, including meditation. All that we can do with any spiritual discipline is produce within ourselves something of the silence, the humility, the detachment, the purity of heart, and the indifference which are required if the inner self is to make some shy, unpredictable manifestation of *His* presence.

The Inner Experience

PART 4

The Person of Christ

During his conversion, Merton explored the mystery of Christ not only through reading but also in churches. At the age of eighteen, during a vacation in Rome, he was so captivated by Byzantine mosaics of Christ that he felt the reality of Christ taking root in his mind and heart. Later, as a monk, Merton recognized that Christ's image is in each of us and that the task of the Christian is to uncover the image in ourselves and other people. As we move forward in this endeavor, we each become a new person who is spiritually reformed and one in identity with Christ.

Merton directs us to Christ at the center of the heart. We find our worth by discovering through prayer that we are loved by Christ. Whether we are gazing at images or attending in silent contemplation, Christ should be the center of our prayer life. All forms of prayer—liturgical prayer, meditation, vocal prayer, or centering prayer—nurture our relationship with the source of all truth and life, Jesus Christ. Experiencing divine love in prayer, we grow in the inward presence of Christ and learn to love others more fully.

This chapter begins by identifying Christ as the center of our lives and then explores what it means not only to live in Christ but also to become united with Christ. Merton invites us to find consolation in our own faith in Christ and his indwelling presence.

The True Way of Life

Christianity is first of all a way of life, rather than a way of thought. Merely to study Christian truths and gain intellectual understanding of them is not enough. Indeed, study does not, by itself, bring us to a complete understanding of them. It is only by living the Christian life that we come to understand the full meaning of the Christian message. The meaning of this message is precisely that God has come to dwell in man and to show, in man, that the sorrows, sufferings, and defeats inherent in human existence can never deprive man's life of meaning as long as he is capable of deciding to live as a son of God and consents to let God live and triumph in his own heart. This is not merely a matter of individual consolation but of fraternal love. The Christian bears witness to God's love for the world by living a communal life in which the presence of Christ is obscurely manifest in the love of brethren for one another.

One cannot live the Christian life as it is meant to be lived without seeking to be holy. In order to be holy, one must become free from the tyranny and the demands of sin, of lust, of anger, of pride, ambition, injustice, and the spirit of violence. When one sincerely renounces sin and selfish living, one begins to find something of the peace and serenity which come from the awareness that God lives and acts in us. However, the "old man" of sin is not yet dead in us. Soon there begins a new phase of struggle and uncertainty, in which we learn that holiness is not easy, and is not just a matter of will power and good intentions. In this difficult struggle we gain experience of our own limitations and weakness. But we also learn, by experience, that if we trust in the power of God, and seek to imitate His Beloved Son, Jesus Christ, in His passion and His victory, we receive mysterious strength that has no human source. Then we begin to become more closely identified with Christ and to realize, at least in the silence of the heart that loves and trusts Him, that He Himself lives in us and is our strength. Jesus Christ is our new and hidden self. Our true way of life is then to renounce our old external self, with its selfish desires and its illusions, in order that Christ may fully live in us. It is thus that we begin to be truly Christians. For then the new life that began in us sacramentally by Baptism becomes a matter of everyday experience, since Christ takes possession of our being in order that He Himself may be life, holiness, and wisdom in us.

. . . To be a Christian is then not only to believe in Christ, but to live as Christ and, in a mysterious way, to become united with Christ. This is both Christian life and Christian holiness.

The way of Christian holiness is then not a way of extraordinary virtue and of miraculous powers, but of simple fidelity and love in the ordinary life of every day. The work, the family life, the simple consolations, and the ordinary sufferings of Christians are lived in a new Spirit, and filled with love and faith that seek only God's will, not personal profit and gratification.

Honorable Reader

Picturing Christ

For some people it is quite easy to turn within themselves and find a simple picture of Christ in their imagination, and this is an easy beginning of prayer. But for others this does not succeed. On the contrary, the effort it costs may fill their heads with problems and disturbances that make prayer impossible. Yet at the same time the mere name of Jesus or the indistinct, unanalyzed notion of Christ is enough to keep their faith fully occupied in a simple and loving awareness of Him Who is really present in our souls by the gift of His Personal love and by His Divine Mission.

This loving awareness is a thing more real and more valuable by far than anything we can arrive at by our interior senses alone, for the picture of Jesus we may have in our imagination remains nothing but a picture, while the love that His grace produces in our hearts can bring us into direct contact with Him as He really is. For Jesus Himself causes this love to spring up within us, by a direct and personal effect of His will. When He touches our souls with His love, He affects us even more directly and intimately than a material object moves and affects our eyes or our other senses. Besides, the only real reason why we meditate on Jesus and reflect on the images of Him in our memory is in order that we may be prepared for this more intimate contact with Him by love. Therefore, when His love begins to burn within us, there is surely no strict necessity for using our imaginations any more. Some may like to, some may not, and others have no choice, one way or another. Use whatever helps you, and avoid what gets in your way.

New Seeds of Contemplation

Souls Are Like Wax

Souls are like wax waiting for a seal. By themselves they have no special identity. Their destiny is to be softened and prepared in this life, by God's will, to receive, at their death, the seal of their own degree of likeness to God in Christ.

And this is what it means, among other things, to be judged by Christ.

The wax that has melted in God's will can easily receive the stamp of its identity, the truth of what it was meant to be. But the wax that is hard and dry and brittle and without love will not take the seal: for the hard seal, descending upon it, grinds it to powder.

Therefore, if you spend your life trying to escape from the heat of the fire that is meant to soften and prepare you to become your true self, and if you try to keep your substance from melting in the fire—as if your true identity were to be hard wax—the seal will fall upon you at last and crush you. You will not be able to take your own true name and countenance, and you will be destroyed by the event that was meant to be your fulfillment.

New Seeds of Contemplation

Understanding Suffering

Suffering, and the consecration it demands, cannot be understood perfectly outside the context of Baptism. For Baptism, in giving us our identity, gives us a divine vocation to find ourselves in Christ. It gives us our identity in Christ. But both the grace and character of Baptism give our soul a spiritual conformity to Christ *in His sufferings*. For Baptism is the application to our souls of the Passion of Christ.

Baptism engrafts us into the mystical vine which is the body of Christ, and makes us live in His life and ripen like grapes on the trellis of His Cross. It brings us into the communion of saints whose life flows from the Passion of Jesus. But every sacrament of union is also a sacrament of separation. In making us members of one another, Baptism also more clearly distinguishes us, not only from those who do not live in Christ, but also and even especially from one another. For it gives us our personal, incommunicable vocation to reproduce in our own lives the life and sufferings and charity of Christ in a way unknown to anyone else who has ever lived under the sun.

. . . Suffering, therefore, must make sense to us not as a vague universal necessity, but as something demanded by our own personal destiny. When I see my trials not as the collision of my life with a blind machine called fate, but as a sacramental gift of Christ's love, given to me by God the Father along with my identity and my very name, then I can consecrate them and myself with them to God. For then I realize that my suffering is not my own. It is the Passion of Christ, stretching out its tendrils into my life in order to bear rich clusters of grapes. . . .

No Man Is an Island

The Love of Jesus

There is no spiritual life outside the love of Christ. We have a spiritual life only because we are loved by Him. The spiritual life consists in receiving the gift of the Holy Spirit and His charity, because the Sacred Heart of Jesus has willed in His love that we should live by His Spirit—the same Spirit which proceeds from the Word and from the Father, and Who is Jesus' love for the Father.

If we know how great is the love of Jesus for us we will never be afraid to go to Him in all our poverty, all our weakness, all our spiritual wretchedness and infirmity. Indeed, when we understand the true nature of His love for us, we will prefer to come to Him poor and helpless. We will never be ashamed of our distress. Distress is to our advantage when we have nothing to seek but mercy. We can be glad of our helplessness when we really believe that His power is made perfect in our infirmity.

The surest sign that we have received a spiritual understanding of God's love for us is the appreciation of our own poverty in the light of His infinite mercy.

Thoughts in Solitude

Photograph of Thomas Merton by John Howard Griffin. Used with permission of the Merton Legacy Trust and the Estate of John Howard Griffin.

PART 5

Prayer of the Heart

Merton wrote little about his personal experience of prayer, but perhaps this was unnecessary because he was clear about a way of prayer that he called "prayer of the heart" or contemplative prayer. Prayer of the heart may use few words or none, but it requires faith and a willing, attentive heart. Trust, joy, loving attention, expectation—not a particular prayer technique—become primary. This prayer entails awakening to the depths of our being, perhaps by invoking the name of Jesus in wonder and love, and resting in the God who is our center.

Merton taught that simply walking with God is one of the surest ways of developing a life of prayer. Prayer such as this unveils the presence of God everywhere; God in the everydayness of life, in the body, in nature, and in the people we encounter. He saw all occasions as opportunities for prayer: preparing a meal, working in a garden, reading a book, taking a walk in the woods, playing with children—all these can be undertaken with a sense of divine presence.

Contemplative prayer reorients our lives to God and reminds us of our need for ongoing conversion and divine mercy. Prayer of the heart grows out of the quality of one's life as a whole and immeasurably nourishes one's life in return.

The following chapter calls us to awaken to the "seeds of contemplation" in the midst of our daily life. One of the signs of God's grace at work in our hearts is that we become aware of the divine in all aspects of life. According to Merton, remembering God through contemplation is at the same time remembering our identity in God. 🌿

An Education of the Heart

For us, the education of a monastic person is the education of the heart. The novitiate formation should be the formation of the heart to know God. This is a very important concept in the contemplative life, both in Sufism and in the Christian tradition: to develop a heart that knows God, not just a heart that loves God, but a heart that knows God. How does one know God in the heart? By praying in the heart. The Sufis have ways of learning to pray so that you are really praying in the heart, from the heart, not just saying words, not just thinking good thoughts or making intentions or acts of the will, but from the heart. This is a very ancient Biblical concept that is carried over from Jewish thought into monasticism.

Thomas Merton in Alaska

The Primacy of Love

Even though one may be a learned man and may have profound knowledge of many subjects, and many "words," this is of no value; it has no central meaning, if the One Word, Love, has not been heard. That One Word is heard only in the silence and solitude of an empty heart, the selfless, undivided heart, the heart that is at peace, detached, free, without care. In the language of Christianity, this freedom is the realm of faith, and hope, but above all of Love. "If I have perfect faith . . . but no Love, I am nothing" (1 Corinthians 13:2).

Honorable Reader

The Real Purpose of Prayer

Real Christian living is stunted and frustrated if it remains content with the bare externals of worship, with "saying prayers" and "going to church," with fulfilling one's external duties and merely being respectable. The real purpose of prayer . . . is the deepening of personal realization in love, the awareness of God (even if sometimes this awareness may amount to a negative factor, a seeming "absence"). The real purpose of meditation—or at least that which recommends itself as most relevant for modern man—is the exploration and discovery of new dimensions in freedom, illumination, and love, in deepening our awareness of our life in Christ.

What is the relation of this to action? Simply this. He who attempts to act and do things for others or for the world without deepening his own self-understanding, freedom, integrity, and capacity to love, will not have anything to give others. He will communicate to them nothing but the contagion of his own obsessions, his aggressiveness, his ego-centered ambitions, his delusions about ends and means, his doctrinaire prejudices and ideas.

Contemplation in a World of Action

Contemplation Is a Response to a Call

Contemplation is also the response to a call: a call from Him Who has no voice, and yet Who speaks in everything that is, and Who, most of all, speaks in the depths of our own being: for we ourselves are words of His. But we are words that are meant to respond to Him, to answer to Him, to echo Him, and even in some way to contain Him and signify

Him. Contemplation is this echo. It is a deep resonance in the inmost center of our spirit in which our very life loses its separate voice and re-sounds with the majesty and the mercy of the Hidden and Living One. He answers Himself in us and this answer is divine life, divine creativity, making all things new. We ourselves become His echo and His answer. It is as if in creating us God asked a question, and in awakening us to contemplation He answered the question, so that the contemplative is, at the same time, question and answer.

New Seeds of Contemplation

What If I Never Think of Him?

Although God lives in the souls of men who are unconscious of Him, how can I say that I have found Him and found myself in Him if I never know Him or think of Him, never take any interest in Him or seek Him or desire His presence in my soul? What good does it do to say a few formal prayers to Him and then turn away and give all my mind and all my will to created things, desiring only ends that fall far short of Him? Even though my soul may be justified, yet if my mind does not belong to Him then I do not belong to Him either. If my love does not reach out toward Him but scatters itself in His creation, it is because I have reduced His life in me to the level of a formality, forbidding it to move me with a truly vital influence.

Justify my soul, O God, but also from Your fountains fill my will with fire. Shine in my mind, although perhaps this means "be darkness to my experience," but occupy my heart with Your tremendous Life. Let my eyes see nothing in the world but Your glory, and let my hands touch nothing that is not for Your service.

New Seeds of Contemplation

Every Moment Plants Something in the Soul

Every moment and every event of every man's life on earth plants something in his soul. For just as the wind carries thousands of winged seeds, so each moment brings with it germs of spiritual vitality that come to rest imperceptibly in the minds and wills of men. Most of these unnumbered seeds perish and are lost, because men are not prepared to receive them: for such seeds as these cannot spring up anywhere except in the good soil of freedom, spontaneity, and love.

This is no new idea. Christ in the parable of the sower long ago told us that "The seed is the word of God." We often think this applies only to the word of the Gospel as formally preached in churches on Sundays. . . . But every expression of the will of God is in some sense a "word" of God and therefore a "seed" of new life. The ever-changing reality in the midst of which we live should awaken us to the possibility of an uninterrupted dialogue with God. By this I do not mean continuous "talk," . . . but a dialogue of love and of choice. A dialogue of deep wills.

New Seeds of Contemplation

Prayer Is More than Words

In meditative prayer, one thinks and speaks not only with his mind and lips, but in a certain sense with his *whole being*.

Prayer is then not just a formula of words, or a series of desires springing up in the heart—it is the orientation of our whole body, mind, and spirit to God in silence, attention, and adoration. All good meditative prayer is a *conversion of our entire self to God.*

One cannot then enter into meditation, in this sense, without a kind of inner upheaval. By upheaval I do not mean a disturbance, but a breaking out of routine, a liberation of the heart from the cares and preoccupations of one's daily business.

Thoughts in Solitude

Rebelling against Contemplation

We must face the fact that the mere thought of contemplation is one which deeply troubles the person who takes it seriously. It is so contrary to the modern way of life, so apparently alien, so seemingly impossible, that the modern man who even considers it finds, at first, that his whole being rebels against it. If the ideal of inner peace remains attractive, the demands of the way to peace seem to be so exacting and so extreme that they can no longer be met. We would like to be quiet, but our restlessness will not allow it. Hence we believe that for us there can be no peace except in a life filled up with movement and activity, with speech, news, communication, recreation, distraction. We seek the meaning of our life in activity for its own sake, activity without objective, efficacy without fruit, scientism, the cult of unlimited power, the service of the machine as an end in itself. And in all these a certain dynamism is imagined. . . .

The reason for this inner confusion and conflict is that our technological society has no longer any place in it for wisdom that seeks truth for its own sake, that seeks fullness of being, that seeks to rest in an intuition of the very ground of all being. Without wisdom, the apparent opposition of action and contemplation, of work and rest, of involvement and detachment, can never be resolved.

Honorable Reader

Just Smell a Flower in the Garden

Better just to smell a flower in the garden or something like that than to have an unauthentic experience of a much higher value. Better to honestly enjoy the sunshine or some light reading than to claim to be in contact with something that one is not in contact with at all.

So, therefore, I would say that it is very important in the contemplative life *not to overemphasize the contemplation.* If we constantly overemphasize those things to which access is inevitably quite rare, we overlook the ordinary authentic real experiences of everyday life as real things to enjoy, things to be happy about, things to praise God for. But the ordinary realities of everyday life, the faith and love with which we live our normal human lives, provide the foundation on which we build those higher things. If there is no foundation, then we have nothing at all! How can we relish the higher things of God if we cannot enjoy some simple little thing that comes along as a gift from Him!

Contemplation in a World of Action

Prayer and Work

Of course where people go wrong is that they fail to realize that this simple prayer can go on even though one may be at work. This state of attention to God certainly can co-exist with a simple kind of action, and the fact that one is not aware of attending to God is perhaps better. It is not necessarily the best and most healthy thing for a person to be sitting quietly, intensely aware of himself as passive. It is better for a person to be somewhat active and not to be aware that anything special is going on, provided that there is no absorption in anything else.

Take the activity of sweeping the floor or washing dishes or chopping wood or cutting grass or something like that. These activities are not distracting. We do not become absorbed in them and it is quite possible to engage in them without any sense that we are praying or that we are doing anything other than simply doing what we do in such a way that we remain quietly close to God. Now, the point I am trying to get to is this: what this attentiveness to God really means is not just a particular psychological state or a peculiar kind of recollection, but it is part and parcel of the experience of love in everyday life.

Contemplation in a World of Action

Expecting an Answer

Cowardice keeps us "double minded"—hesitating between the world and God. In this hesitation, there is no true faith—faith remains an opinion. We are never certain, because we never quite give in to the authority of an invisible God. This hesitation is the death of hope. We never let go of those visible supports which, we well know, must one day surely fail us. And this hesitation makes true prayer impossible—it never quite dares to ask for anything, or if it asks, it is so uncertain of being heard that in the very act of asking it surreptitiously seeks by human prudence to construct a make-shift answer (cf. James 1:5-8).

What is the use of praying, if at the very moment of prayer, we have so little confidence in God that we are busy planning our own kind of answer to our prayer?

Thoughts in Solitude

Yearning for the Presence of God

In the "prayer of the heart" we seek first of all the deepest ground of our identity in God. We do not reason about dogmas of faith, or "the mysteries." We seek rather to gain a direct existential grasp, a personal experience of the deepening truths of life and faith, *finding ourselves in God's truth.* . . . Prayer then means yearning for the simple presence of God, for a personal understanding of his word, for knowledge of his will and for capacity to hear and obey him. It is thus something much more than uttering petitions for good things external to our own deepest concerns.

The Climate of Monastic Prayer

Like Spokes to the Center of a Wheel

This is the center to which everything else must go just like the spokes go to the center of a wheel. If we do not keep the center in mind and if we do not live in this center, everything then becomes a rat race.

What leads you into this center is a life of prayer. At this center you will experience the love and mercy of God for yourself and find your true identity as a person to whom God has been merciful and continues to be merciful.

What leads up to this discovery is self-knowledge. I must find myself. I must solve my identity crisis, if I have one, then find myself as one loved by God, as chosen by God, and visited and overshadowed by God's mercy, which I now experience as totally in terms of God's mercy.

This, of course, implies that in relation to my brother he also enjoys the same kind of identity at the center of his being. This is what the story of the Bible is all about, this is the ultimate secret that came forth from the Father and is manifested in Christ, the love and mercy of God has built its tent among us in Jesus Christ and communicates to us in Spirit.

This is what the life of prayer is for. Prayer has to break into this depth where this realization of God's mystery is also an act of obedience whereby we accept ourselves as totally given; that is, that all we have comes from the Father. This is what it means to be Christ-like because this was the life of the Son of God on earth.

Thomas Merton in Alaska

All Prayer Is Communion

All prayer is communion, not only between Christ and me but also between everybody in the Church and myself. All prayer takes us into the communion of saints. Perhaps it would be helpful to think that when I am praying I am closely united with everybody who ever prayed and everybody now praying. I am completely caught up in this communion of saints and this great reality of the prayer of Christ. I am not lost or submerged in it, but I am truly myself when I am praying in union with Christ and with the communion of saints.

Thomas Merton in Alaska

God Has Chosen Us

Contemplation is really simple openness to God at every moment, and deep peace. And when you say "experience the mysteries of Christ," it just means a deep realization in the very depths of our being that God has chosen and loved us from all eternity, that we really are His children and we really are loved by Him, that there really is a personal bond and He really is present. This is so simple that there is no need to make a commotion about it.

Thomas Merton in Alaska

What About Distractions?

What do you do with distractions? You either simply let them pass by and ignore them, or you let them pass by and be perfectly content to have them. If you don't pay any attention to them, the distractions don't remain. They are like dreams. All you have to do is go to sleep and everything starts going through your mind, but you don't realize it, you only remember part of it. . . .

So if you are getting distractions what you do is to say, "Oh, there goes the Union Pacific; that is my grandmother," and so on. You just note it—there it is. Gradually you become aware, "I am having a distraction about this," but it is not the ultimate, it is just something you become conscious of. When you are fully able to note distractions and see them going by, then you are in a position to make a choice. You can observe them and say, "I didn't choose to have this go by here," or "It is inevitable to have this go by here." You become aware of the fact that the distraction is not really yours. And once you are aware of that, you cannot be bothered by them because distractions only cause confusion when you are in doubt.

Thomas Merton in Alaska

PART 6

Solitude and Silence

Merton realized that solitude and silence are essential for all people who seek to be intimate with God, because they allow us to answer a call at the center of the heart. This call is to listen to the voice of God, to hear and to pray—not later, but now.

Merton taught that inner solitude allows no room for self-preoccupation; we are invited to forget ourselves in the presence of God and to sacrifice our hidden agendas for God's plan. In solitude the illusion that we can exist separately from God is shattered. Rather, we are invited to stay with feelings of emptiness and loneliness—not escape through distractions or talk—but sink within, allowing ourselves to be transformed. In our loneliness, according to Merton, we discover that God longs to be alone in us. God's gift is love—this is the reason we need to be faithful to solitude.

Throughout his life Merton was drawn to silence and, in the monastery, basked in the silence of the woods. His quest for silence led beyond the mere absence of sound. Outward silence opens the door to inner silence; and inner silence is the silence of the true self before God. In its deepest form, this inner silence eschews thoughts and words and makes us simply present, listening, attending to God and our true self. In other words, inner silence permits encounter with the innermost, true self that is obscure, hidden, and veiled. It is a gift God gives when we are ready to listen and attend.

Rather than hinder our relationship with others, solitude and silence nurture love and communion. For Merton, those who answer the call to solitude and silence find themselves participating in a human dimension shared by all. As a result, in the depths of our lives we find a compassionate bond with all people, one that enriches every aspect of our lives and nurtures authentic community.

These selections begin with a description of true solitude and what it means for the inner life as well as our shared lives. Merton invites us to think of solitude not as something we choose but as a call of love that draws us out of ourselves. The latter group of selections addresses the power of silence beyond words and what it means to fill our lives with silence. The descriptions of solitude and silence weave together, calling us back to our longing to center our lives solely on God's love.

I Love This Solitude

My chief joy is to escape to the attic of the garden house and the little broken window that looks out over the valley. There in the silence I love the green grass. The tortured gestures of the apple trees have become part of my prayer. I look at the shining water under the willows and listen to the sweet songs of all the living things that are in our woods and fields. So much do I love this solitude that when I walk out along the road to the old barns that stand alone, far from the new buildings, delight begins to overpower me from head to foot and peace smiles even in the marrow of my bones.

The Sign of Jonas

An Abyss Opening Up in Our Souls

The truest solitude is not something outside you, not an absence of men or of sound around you; it is an abyss opening up in the center of your own soul.

And this abyss of interior solitude is a hunger that will never be satisfied with any created thing.

The only way to find solitude is by hunger and thirst and sorrow and poverty and desire, and the man who has found solitude is empty, as if he had been emptied by death.

He has advanced beyond all horizons. There are no directions left in which he can travel. This is a country whose center is everywhere and whose circumference is nowhere. You do not find it by traveling but by standing still.

Yet it is in this loneliness that the deepest activities begin. It is here that you discover act without motion, labor that is profound repose, vision in obscurity, and, beyond all desire, a fulfillment whose limits extend to infinity. . . .

There should be at least a room, or some corner where no one will find you and disturb you or notice you. You should be able to untether yourself from the world and set yourself free, loosing all the fine strings and strands of tension that bind you, by sight, by sound, by thought, to the presence of other men.

New Seeds of Contemplation

Taking Responsibility for the Inner Life

One of the first essentials of the interior solitude of which I speak is that it is the actualization of a faith in which a man takes responsibility for his own inner life. He faces its full mystery, in the presence of the invisible God. And he takes upon himself the lonely, barely comprehensible, incommunicable task of working his way through the darkness of his own mystery until he discovers that his mystery and the mystery of God merge into one reality, which is the only reality. That God lives in him and he in God. . . .

. . . Without solitude of some sort there is and can be no maturity. Unless one becomes empty and alone, he cannot give himself in love because he does not possess the deep self which is the only gift worthy of love. And this deep self, we immediately add, cannot be *possessed*. My deep self is not "something" which I acquire, or to which I "attain" after a long struggle. It is not mine, and cannot be mine. It is no "thing"—no object. It is "I."

The shallow "I" of individualism can be possessed, developed, cultivated, pandered to, satisfied: it is the center of all our strivings for gain and for satisfaction, whether material or spiritual. But the deep "I" of the spirit, of solitude and of love, cannot be "had," possessed, developed, perfected. It can only *be*, and *act* according to deep inner laws which are not of man's contriving, but which come from God. They are the Laws of the Spirit, who, like the wind, blows where He wills. This inner "I," who is always alone, is always universal: for in this inmost "I" my own solitude meets the solitude of every other man and the solitude of God. Hence it is beyond division, beyond limitations, beyond selfish affirmation. It is only this inmost solitary "I" that truly loves with the love and the Spirit of Christ. This "I" is Christ Himself, living in us: and we, in Him, living in the Father.

Disputed Questions

Solitude Is Shared by Everyone

Even though he may be physically alone, the solitary remains united to others and lives in profound solidarity with them, but on a deeper and mystical level. They may think he is one with them in the vain interests and preoccupations of a superficial social existence. He realizes that he is one with them in the peril and anguish of their common solitude: not the solitude of the individual only, but the radical and essential *solitude of man*—a solitude which was assumed by Christ and which, in Christ, becomes mysteriously identified with the solitude of God.

The solitary is one who is aware of solitude in himself as a basic and inevitable human reality, not just as something which affects him as an isolated individual. Hence his solitude is the foundation of a deep, pure and gentle sympathy with all other men, whether or not they are capable of realizing the tragedy of their plight. More—it is the doorway by which he enters into the mystery of God, and brings others into that mystery by the power of his love and his humility.

Disputed Questions

Find Moments of Relaxation

In the interior life there should be moments of relaxation, freedom, and "browsing." Perhaps the best way to do this is in the midst of nature, but also in literature. Perhaps also a certain amount of art is necessary, and music. Of course we have to remember our time is limited and first things have to come first. We can't spend too much time just listening to music.

You also need a good garden, and you need access to the woods, or to the sea. Get out in those hills and really be in the midst of nature a little bit! That is not only legitimate, it is in a certain way necessary.

. . . When you are by yourself you soon get tired of your craziness. It is too exhausting. It does not fit in with the eminent sanity of trees, birds, water, sky. You have to shut up and go about the business of living. The silence of the woods forces you to make a decision which the tensions and artificialities of society may help you to evade forever. Do you want to be yourself or don't you?

Contemplation in a World of Action

Respecting the Spiritual Privacy of Others

Secrecy and solitude are values that belong to the very essence of personality.

A person is a person insofar as he has a secret and is a solitude of his own that cannot be communicated to anyone else. If I love a person, I will love that which most makes him a person: the secrecy, the hiddenness, the solitude of his own individual being, which God alone can penetrate and understand.

A love that breaks into the spiritual privacy of another in order to lay open all his secrets and besiege his solitude with importunity does not love him: it seeks to destroy what is best in him, and what is most intimately his.

No Man Is an Island

True and False Solitude

True solitude is found in humility, which is infinitely rich. False solitude is the refuge of pride, and it is infinitely poor. The poverty of false solitude comes from an illusion which pretends, by adorning itself in things it can never possess, to distinguish one individual self from the mass of other men. True solitude is selfless. Therefore, it is rich in silence and charity and peace. It finds in itself seemingly inexhaustible resources of good to bestow on other people. False solitude is self-centered. And because it finds nothing in its own center, it seeks to draw all things into itself. But everything it touches becomes infected with its own nothingness, and falls apart. True solitude cleans the soul, lays it wide open to the four winds of generosity. False solitude locks the door against all men and pores over its own private accumulation of rubbish.

No Man Is an Island

Entering the Darkness of the Inner Self

The truly sacred attitude toward life is in no sense an escape from the sense of nothingness that assails us when we are left alone with ourselves. On the contrary, it penetrates into that darkness and that nothingness, realizing that the mercy of God has transformed our nothingness into His temple and believing that in our darkness His light has hidden itself. Hence the sacred attitude is one which does not recoil from our own inner emptiness, but rather penetrates into it with awe and reverence, and with the awareness of mystery.

This is a most important discovery in the interior life. For the external self *fears* and recoils from what is beyond it and above it. It dreads the seeming emptiness and darkness of the interior self. The whole tragedy of "diversion" is precisely that it is a flight from all that is most real and immediate and genuine in ourselves. It is a flight from life and from experience—an attempt to put a veil of objects between the mind and its experience of itself. It is therefore a matter of great courage and spiritual energy to turn away from diversion and prepare to meet, face-to-face, that *immediate* experience of life which is intolerable to the exterior man. This is only possible when, by a gift of God, . . . we are able to see our inner selves not as a vacuum but as an *infinite depth,* not as emptiness but as fullness. This change of perspective is impossible as long as we are afraid of our own nothingness, as long as we are afraid of fear, afraid of poverty, afraid of boredom—as long as we run away from ourselves.

The Inner Experience

The Ground of Life

Is it true to say that one goes into solitude to "get at the root of existence"? It would be better simply to say that in solitude one *is* at the root. He who is alone, and is conscious of what his solitude means, finds himself simply in the ground of life. He is "in Love." He is in love with all, with everyone, with everything. He is not surprised at this, and he is able to live with this disconcerting and unexciting reality, which has no explanation. He lives, then, as a seed planted in the ground. As Christ said, the seed in the ground must die. To be as a seed in the ground of one's very life is to dissolve in that ground in order to become fruitful. One disappears into

Love, in order to "be Love." But this fruitfulness is beyond any planning and any understanding of man. To be "fruitful" in this sense, one must forget every idea of fruitfulness or productivity, and merely *be*.

Love and Living

A True and Special Vocation

Vocation to Solitude—To deliver oneself up, to hand oneself over, entrust oneself completely to the silence of a wide landscape of woods and hills, or sea, or desert; to sit still while the sun comes up over that land and fills its silences with light. To pray and work in the morning and to labor and rest in the afternoon, and to sit still again in meditation in the evening when night falls upon that land and when the silence fills itself with darkness and with stars. This is a true and special vocation. There are few who are willing to belong completely to such silence, to let it soak into their bones, to breathe nothing but silence, to feed on silence, and to turn the very substance of their life into a living and vigilant silence.

Thoughts in Solitude

Desert Solitude

The Desert Fathers believed that the wilderness had been created as supremely valuable in the eyes of God precisely because it had no value to men. The wasteland was the land that could never be wasted by men because it offered them nothing. There was nothing to attract them. There was nothing to exploit. The desert was the region in which the Chosen

People had wandered for forty years, cared for by God alone. They could have reached the Promised Land in a few months if they had traveled directly to it. God's plan was that they should always look back upon the time in the desert as the idyllic time of their life with Him alone.

The desert was created simply to be itself, not to be transformed by men into something else. So too the mountain and the sea. The desert is therefore the logical dwelling place for the man who seeks to be nothing but himself—that is to say, a creature solitary and poor and dependent upon no one but God.

Thoughts in Solitude

The Word Emerges from Silence

Christianity is a religion of the Word. The Word is Love. But we sometimes forget that the Word emerges first of all from silence. When there is no silence, then the One Word which God speaks is not truly heard as Love. Then only "words" are heard. "Words" are not love, for they are many and Love is One. Where there are many words, we lose consciousness of the fact that there is really only One Word. The One Word which God speaks is Himself. Speaking, he manifests Himself as infinite Love. His speaking and His hearing are One. So silent is His speech that, to our way of thinking, His speech is no speech, His hearing is no-hearing. Yet in his silence, in the abyss of His one Love, all words are spoken and all words are heard. Only in this silence of infinite Love do they have coherence and meaning.

Honorable Reader

The Undivided Heart

Even though one may be a learned man and may have profound knowledge of many subjects, and many "words," this is of no value; it has no central meaning, if the One Word, Love, has not been heard. That One Word is heard only in the silence and solitude of the empty heart, the selfless, undivided heart, the heart that is at peace, detached, free, without care. In the language of Christianity, this freedom is the realm of faith, and hope, but above all of Love.

Honorable Reader

The Silent Self Within

There is a silent self within us whose presence is disturbing precisely because it is so silent: it *can't* be spoken. It has to remain silent. To articulate it, to verbalize it, is to tamper with it, and in some ways to destroy it.

Now let us frankly face the fact that our culture is one which is geared in many ways to help us evade any need to face this inner, silent self. We live in a state of constant semi-attention to the sound of voices, music, traffic, or the generalized noise of what goes on around us all the time. This keeps us immersed in a flood of racket and words, a diffuse medium in which our consciousness is half diluted: we are not quite "thinking," not entirely responding, but we are more or less there. We are not fully *present* and not entirely absent; not fully withdrawn, yet not completely available. . . . .

Of course this is not enough to keep us completely forgetful of the other unwelcome self that remains so largely unconscious. The disquieting presence of our deep self keeps forcing its way almost to the surface of awareness. To exorcise this presence we need a more definite stimulation, a distraction, a drink, a drug, a gimmick, a game, a routine of acting out our sense of alienation and trouble. Then it goes away for the time being and we forget who we are.

All of this can be described as "noise," as commotion and jamming which drown out the deep, secret, and insistent demands of the inner self.

With this inner self we have to come to terms *in silence.* That is the reason for choosing silence. In silence we face and admit the gap between the depths of our being, which we consistently ignore, and the surface which is untrue to our own reality. We recognize the need to be at home with ourselves in order that we may go out to meet others, not just with a mask of affability, but with real commitment and authentic love.

If we are afraid of being alone, afraid of silence, it is perhaps because of our secret despair of inner reconciliation. If we have no hope of being at peace with ourselves in our own personal loneliness and silence, we will never be able to face ourselves at all: we will keep running and never stop.

Love and Living

In the Silence of the Hermitage

There was a heavy rain all night. Now the rain on the roof accentuates the silence and surrounds the dryness and light of the hermitage as though with love and peace. The liberty and tranquility of this place are indescribable, more than any bodily peace. This is a gift of God marked with His simplicity and His purity. How one's heart opens and what hope arises in the core of my being! It is as if I had not really hoped in God for years, as if I had been living all this time in despair.

. . . Everything about this hermitage fills me with gladness. There are lots of things that could have been far more perfect one way or the other, ascetically or domestically, but it is the place God has given me after so much prayer and longing and without my deserving it, and it is a delight. I can imagine no other joy on earth than to have such a place to be at peace in. To live in silence, to think and write, to listen to the wind and to all the voices of the wood, to struggle with a new anguish, which is, nevertheless, blessed and secure, to live in the shadow of a big cedar cross, to prepare for my death and my exodus to the heavenly country, to love my brothers and all people, to pray for the whole world and offer peace and good sense among men. So it is my place in the scheme of things and that is sufficient. Amen.

A Vow of Conversation

The Depths of Silence

There is in all things an inexhaustible sweetness and purity, a silence that is a fount of action and joy. It rises up in wordless gentleness and flows out to me from the unseen roots of all created being, welcoming me tenderly, saluting me with indescribable humility. This is at once my own being, my own nature, and the Gift of my Creator's Thought and Art within me, speaking as Hagia Sophia, speaking as my sister, Wisdom.

The Collected Poems of Thomas Merton

Filling Our Lives with Silence

If our life is poured out in useless words we will never hear anything in the depths of our hearts, where Christ lives and speaks in silence. We will never be anything, and in the end, when the time comes for us to declare who and what we are, we shall be found speechless at the moment of the crucial decision: for we shall have said everything and exhausted ourselves in speech before we had anything to say.

There must be a time of day when the man who makes plans forgets his plans, and acts as if he had no plans at all.

There must be a time of day when the man who has to speak falls very silent. And his mind forms no more propositions, and he asks himself: Did they have a meaning?

There must be a time when the man of prayer goes to pray as if it were the first time in his life he had ever prayed; when the man of resolutions puts his resolutions aside as if they had all been broken, and he learns a different wisdom: distinguishing the sun from the moon, the stars from the darkness, the sea from the dry land, and the night sky from the shoulder of a hill.

No Man Is an Island

The Sky Is My Prayer

When I am liberated by silence, when I am no longer involved in the measurement of life, but in the living of it, I can discover a form of prayer in which there is, effectively, no distraction. My whole life becomes a prayer. My whole silence is full of prayer. The world of silence in which I am immersed contributes to my prayer. . . .

Let me seek, then, the gift of silence, and poverty, and solitude, where everything I touch is turned into prayer: where the sky is my prayer, the birds are my prayer, the wind in the trees is my prayer, for God is all in all.

Thoughts in Solitude

Silence between Words

For language to have meaning, there must be intervals of silence somewhere, to divide word from word and utterance from utterance. He who retires into silence does not necessarily hate language. Perhaps it is love and respect for language which impose silence upon him. For the mercy of God is not heard in words unless it is heard, both before and after the words are spoken, in silence.

Disputed Questions

Thomas Merton on his ordination day, May 26, 1949. Used with permission of the Merton Legacy Trust and the Thomas Merton Center at Bellarmine University.

PART 7

Love of Nature

Merton reveled in the Kentucky landscape of knolls and forests that surrounded the monastery complex. His sacramental vision made him increasingly aware of the seasons as complementary to the liturgy and to the process of death and resurrection in his own spiritual life. Toward the end of his life, in a hermitage on monastery grounds, he envisioned himself at home in the universe and connected in kinship to all creatures—deer, insects, myrtle warblers, raccoons, and frogs. All of nature joined him as he prayed the psalms, and he found his being merging with the sacred and rhythmic dance of all creation.

To express our gratitude for the gifts that we receive, Merton emphasized that we need to purify and further open our hearts to the divine present in all creation. As we attend to God's presence within, we will begin to see the holiness in the world around us. Seeing in this way has power, because we no longer encounter the world only as a physical reality but as a revelation of love. Such seeing has the power to transfigure the world and, at the same time, deepen our respect for nature. We seek harmony with the universe rather than domination, and we walk with a sense that the ground underfoot is truly holy.

How do we draw close to nature? Merton suggests in the selections of this chapter that we open our hearts to the fact that we are part of nature and called to kinship with all. Our vision needs to change, and our eyes need to gaze gently at the beauty around us. In this way we transform ourselves and the world around us.

The Importance of Place

Returning to the monastery from the hospital: cool evening, gray sky, the dark hills. Once again I get the strange sense that one has when he comes back to the place that has been chosen for him by Providence. I belong to this parcel of land with rocky rills around it, with pine trees on it. These are the woods and fields that I have worked in, and walked in, and in which I have encountered the deepest mystery of my own life. And in a sense I never chose this place for myself, it was chosen for me (though of course one must ratify the choice by a personal decision).

Conjectures of a Guilty Bystander

A Spring Morning in the Woods

A spring morning alone in the woods. Sunrise: the enormous yolk of energy spreading and spreading as if to take over the entire sky. After that: the ceremonies of the birds feeding in the wet grass. The meadow lark, feeding and singing. Then the quiet, totally silent, dry, sun-drenched mid-morning of spring, under the climbing sun. April is not the cruelest month. Not in Kentucky. It was hard to say Psalms. Attention would get carried away in the vast blue arc of the sky, trees, hills, grass, and all things. How absolutely central is the truth that we are first of all *part of nature*, though we are a very special part, that which is conscious of God. In solitude, one is entirely surrounded by beings which perfectly obey God. This leaves only one place open for me, and if I occupy that place then I, too, am fulfilling His will. The place nature "leaves open" belongs to the conscious one, the one who is aware, who sees all this as a unity, who offers it all to God in praise, joy, thanks. To me, these are not "spiritual acts" or special virtues, but rather the simple, normal, obvious functions of man, without which it is hard to see how he can be human. . . . One has to be alone, under the sky, before everything falls into place and one finds his own place in the midst of it all.

Conjectures of a Guilty Bystander

Come Alive to Beauty

One of the most important—and most neglected—elements in the beginnings of the interior life is the ability to respond to reality, to see the value and the beauty in ordinary things, to come alive to the splendor that is all around us in the creatures of God.

. . . All nature is meant to make us think of paradise. Woods, fields, valleys, hills, the rivers and the sea, the clouds traveling across the sky, light and darkness, sun and stars, remind us that the world was first created as a paradise for the first Adam, and that in spite of his sin and ours, it will once again become a paradise when we are all risen from death in the second Adam. Heaven is even now mirrored in created things. All God's creatures invite us to forget our vain cares and enter into our own hearts, which God Himself has made to be His paradise and our own. If we have God dwelling within us, making our souls His paradise, then the world around us can also become for us what it was meant to be for Adam—his paradise.

No Man Is an Island

Landscape Is Important for Prayer

Since the sun was higher than it usually is in that interval I saw the country in a light that we usually do not see. The low-slanting rays picked out the foliage of the trees and high-lighted a new wheatfield against the dark curtain of woods on the knobs, that were in shadow. It was very beautiful. Deep peace. Sheep on the slopes behind the sheep barn. The new trellises in the novitiate garden leaning and sagging under a hill of roses. A cardinal singing suddenly in the walnut tree, and piles of fragrant logs all around the woodshed waiting to be cut in bad weather.

I looked at all this in great tranquility, with my soul and spirit quiet. For me, landscape seems to be important for contemplation; anyway, I have no scruples about loving it.

The Sign of Jonas

At Play in the Garden of Creation

What is serious to men is often very trivial in the sight of God. What in God might appear to us as "play" is perhaps what He Himself takes most seriously. At any rate the Lord plays and diverts Himself in the garden of His creation, and if we could let go of our own obsession with what we think is the meaning of it all, we might be able to hear His call and follow Him in His mysterious, cosmic dance. We do not have to go very far to catch echoes of that game, and of that dancing. When we are alone on a starlit night; when by chance we see the migrating birds in autumn descending on a grove of junipers to rest and eat; when we see children in a moment when they are really children; when we know love in our own hearts; or when, like the Japanese poet Basho we hear an old frog land in a quiet pond with a solitary splash—at such times the awakening, the turning inside out of all values, the "newness," the emptiness, and the purity of vision that makes themselves evident, provide a glimpse of the cosmic dance.

New Seeds of Contemplation

A Sense of Total Kinship

In the afternoon, there were lots of pretty little myrtle warblers playing and diving for insects in the low pine branches over my head. So close, I could almost touch them. I was awed at their loveliness, their quick flight, their lookings and chirpings, the yellow spot on the back revealed in flight. A sense of total kinship with them as if they and I were all of the same nature and as if that nature were nothing but love.

Indeed, what else but love keeps us all together in being?

. . . Last evening, when the moon was rising, I saw the warm burning soft red of a doe in the field. It was still light enough, so I got the field glasses and watched her. Presently a stag came out of the woods and then I saw a second doe and then briefly, a second stag. They were not afraid. They looked at me from time to time. I watched their beautiful running, their grazing. . . .

A contemplative intuition, yet this is perfectly ordinary, everyday seeing—what everybody ought to see all the time. The deer reveals to me something essential, not only in itself, but also in myself. Something beyond the trivialities of my everyday being, my individual existence. Something profound. The face of that which is both in the deer and in myself.

A Vow of Conversation

The Universe Is My Home

One thing the hermitage is making me see is that the universe is my home and I am nothing if not part of it. . . . . . Only as part of the world's fabric and dynamism can I find my true being in God, who has willed me to exist in the world. This, I discover here in the hermitage, not mentally only but in depth and wholeness, especially, for instance, in the ability to sleep. At the monastery, frogs kept me awake. There are frogs here but they do not keep me awake. They are a comfort, an extension of my own being. Now the hum of the electric meter near by bed is nothing, though in the monastery it would have been intolerable. So there is an acceptance of nature and even of technology in my true habitat. I do not have to work the thing out *theoretically*. It is working itself out in practice in a way that does not need to be explained or justified.

A Vow of Conversation

In God's Light

I looked up at the clear sky and the tops of the leafless trees shining in the sun and it was a moment of angelic lucidity. I said the Psalms of Tierce with great joy, overflowing joy, as if the land and woods and spring were all praising God through me. Again the sense of angelic transparency of everything: of pure, simple, and total light.

The word that comes closest to pointing to it is "simple." It was all so simple, but with a simplicity to which one seems to aspire, only seldom to attain it. A simplicity that is and has and says everything just because it is simple.

A Vow of Conversation

Rain Is a Festival

The rain I am in is not like the rain of cities. It fills the woods with an immense and confused sound. It covers the flat roof of the cabin and its porch with insistent and controlled rhythms. And I listen, because it reminds me again and again that the world runs by rhythms I have not yet learned to recognize, rhythms that are not those of the engineer.

I came up here from the monastery last night, sloshing through the cornfield, said Vespers, and put some oatmeal on the Coleman stove for supper. It boiled over while I was listening to the rain and toasting a piece of bread at the log fire. The night became very dark. The rain surrounded the whole cabin with its enormous virginal myth, a whole world of meaning, of secrecy, of silence, of rumor. Think of it: all that speech pouring down, selling nothing, judging nobody, drenching the thick mulch of dead leaves, soaking the trees, filling gullies and crannies of the wood with water, washing out the places where men have stripped the hillside! What a thing it is to sit absolutely alone, in the forest, at night, cherished by this wonderful, unintelligible, perfectly innocent speech, the most comforting speech in the world, the talk that rain makes by itself all over the ridges, and the talk of the watercourses everywhere in the hollows!

Raids on the Unspeakable

PART 8

Community Life

According to the testimony of his own Trappist brothers, Merton was well loved in the community and had a special affection for members who went unnoticed. On the day that the news of Merton's death reached Gethsemani (Merton was speaking about monastic renewal at a Bangkok conference), an elderly monk for whom Merton had special affection found a postcard from Merton waiting for him in the refectory.

Merton made it clear that the contemplative life is not isolated but is most fully lived in a reciprocal relationship with a community. Spiritual stability requires sharing in communal life. Even Merton's well-known preference for a hermit's solitude never uprooted him from the ground of religious life.

For Merton, the discovery of God as the authentic center of life coincides with the awakening of our capacity to love other people. The paradox of the contemplative life, for him, was that one cannot move inward with any depth unless one forgets oneself in service to others. This selfless love is one of the fruits of an active prayer life. Our ability to love and serve, then, depends on our willingness to think less of our self-estimation and the estimation of others and, instead, to rely on the deep wellspring of God's life within us. To think that the spiritual life can be separated from people around us is an illusion. We are one body in Christ. We can truly understand and care for other people only by loving the God who knows the depths of our hearts and loves each one of us unconditionally.

The selections in this chapter concentrate on the authentic love necessary for concrete service to others. Merton challenges us to keep in mind one simple idea: that charity withers on the vine unless it is rooted and watered by our relationship with the God who is love.

We All Become Windows

One of the paradoxes of the mystical life is this: *that a man cannot enter into the deepest center of himself and pass through that center into God, unless he is able to pass entirely out of himself and empty himself and give himself to other people in the purity of a selfless love.*

And so one of the worst illusions in the life of contemplation would be to try to find God by barricading yourself inside your own soul, shutting out all external reality by sheer concentration and willpower, cutting yourself off from the world and other men by stuffing yourself inside your own mind and closing the door like a turtle.

. . . Love comes out of God and gathers us to God in order to pour itself back into God through all of us and bring us all back to Him on the tide of His own infinite mercy.

So we all become doors and windows through which God shines back into His own house.

When the Love of God is in me, God is able to love you through me and you are able to love God through me. If my soul were closed to that love, God's love for you and your love for God and God's love for Himself in you and in me, would be denied the particular expression which it finds through me and through no other.

New Seeds of Contemplation

I Must Have Compassion

I cannot treat other men as men unless I have compassion for them. I must have at least enough compassion to realize that when they suffer they feel somewhat as I do when

I suffer. And if for some reason I do not spontaneously feel this kind of sympathy for others, then it is God's will that I do what I can to learn how. I must learn to share with others their joys, their sufferings, their ideas, their needs, their desires. I must learn to do this not only in the cases of those who are of the same class, the same profession, the same race, the same nation as myself, but when men who suffer belong to other groups, even to groups that are regarded as hostile. If I do this, I obey God. If I refuse to do it, I disobey Him.

New Seeds of Contemplation

Believe in the Power of Love

We must all believe in love and in peace. We must believe in the power of love. We must recognize that our being itself is grounded in love: that is to say that we come into being because we are loved and because we are meant to love others. The failure to believe this and to live accordingly creates instead a deep mistrust, a suspicion of others, a hatred of others, a failure to love. When a man attempts to live by and for himself alone, he becomes a little "island" of hate, greed, suspicion, fear, desire. Then his whole outlook on life is falsified. All his judgments are affected by this untruth. In order to recover the true perspective, which is that of love and compassion, he must once again learn, in simplicity, truth, and peace, that "No man is an island."

Honorable Reader

The First Step to Unselfish Love

The first step to unselfish love is the recognition that our love may be deluded. We must first of all purify our love by renouncing the pleasure of loving as an end in itself. As long as pleasure is our end, we will be dishonest with ourselves and with those we love. We will not seek their good, but our own pleasure.

It is clear, then, that to love others well we must first love the truth. And since love is a matter of practical and concrete human relations, the truth we must love when we love our brothers is not mere abstract speculation: it is the moral truth that is to be embodied and given life in our own destiny and theirs. This truth is more than the cold perception of an obligation, flowing from moral precepts. The truth we must love in loving our brothers is the concrete destiny and sanctity that are willed for them by the love of God. One who really loves another is not merely moved by the desire to see him contented and healthy and prosperous in this world. Love cannot be satisfied with anything so incomplete. If I am to love my brother, I must somehow enter deep into the mystery of God's love for him. I must be moved not only by human sympathy but by divine sympathy which is revealed to us in Jesus and which enriches our own lives by the outpouring of the Holy Spirit in our hearts.

No Man Is an Island

Living for Others

It is therefore of supreme importance that we consent to live not for ourselves but for others. When we do this we will be able first of all to face and accept our own limitations. As long as we secretly adore ourselves, our own deficiencies will remain to torture us with an apparent defilement. But if we live for others, we will gradually discover that no one expects us to be "as gods." We will see that we are human, like everyone else, that we all have weaknesses and deficiencies, and that these limitations of ours play a most important part in all our lives. It is because of them that we need others and others need us. We are not all weak in the same spots, and so we supplement and complete one another, each one making up in himself for the lack in another.

Only when we see ourselves in our true human context, as members of a race which is intended to be one organism and "one body," will we begin to understand the positive importance not only of the successes but of the failures and accidents in our lives. My successes are not my own. The way to them was prepared by others. The fruit of my labors is not my own: for I am preparing the way for the achievements of another. Nor are my failures my own. They may spring from the failure of another, but they are also compensated for by another's achievement. Therefore the meaning of my life is not to be looked for merely in the sum total of my own achievements. It is seen only in the complete integration of my achievements and failures with the achievements and failures of my own generation, and society, and time. It is seen, above all, in my integration in the mystery of Christ.

No Man Is an Island

Build Community on God's Love

The ultimate thing is that we build community not on our love but on God's love, because we really do not have that much love ourselves, and that is the real challenge of the religious life. It puts us in a position where sometimes natural community is very difficult. People are sent here and there, and often very incompatible people are thrown together. Groups of people who would never have chosen to be together in an ordinary human way find themselves living together. O.K. This is a test of faith. This puts God's love to the test and it is meant to. It is what St. Paul means. It isn't just a question of whether you are building community with people that you naturally like, it is also a question of building community with people that God has brought together.

Thomas Merton in Alaska

Personality Is Not Individuality

Two Desert Fathers had been living together as hermits for many years and had never gotten into a fight. One of them said to the other, "Why don't we do like everybody else in the world and get into a fight?" The other fellow said, "O.K., how do you do it?" He said, "Well, fights start over possessions, owning something exclusively so that the other fellow can't have it. Let's look around and get ourselves a possession and then have a fight over it." So he found a brick and said, "I will put this brick between us and I will say, 'This is my brick,' and you will immediately say, 'No, it is mine,' and then we will get into a fight." So the man gets the brick and puts it down between the two of them and says, "This is my brick." And the other says, "Well, brother, if it is your brick, take it."

. . .There is a real truth underlying [this story]: if a person is led by the Holy Spirit he no longer has any kind of self that he defends. He is not defending himself, he is going with the Holy Spirit.

We misunderstand personality completely if we think, "My personality is nothing but my little exclusive portion of human nature." Because it isn't. That is my individuality; when I die that individuality has either got to disappear immediately or has to go through purgatory and be gotten rid of there. Personality is not individuality. Individuality is exclusive; personality is not. Each one of us has an individuality which is exclusive, but that is not the whole story, and that is not the person that you are trying to fulfill . . . what the person really is is an existence for others, and the pattern for that is the Trinity.

Thomas Merton in Alaska

The Heresy of Individualism

If I do not have unity in myself, how can I even think, let alone speak, of unity among Christians? Yet, of course, in seeking unity for all Christians, I also attain unity within myself.

The heresy of individualism: thinking oneself a completely self-sufficient unit and asserting this imaginary "unity" against all others. The affirmation of the self as simply "not the other." But when you seek to affirm your unity by denying that you have anything to do with anyone else in the universe until you come down to *you*: what is there left to affirm? Even if there were something to affirm, you would have no breath left with which to affirm it.

The true way is just the opposite: the more I am able to affirm others, to say "yes" to them in myself, by discovering them in myself and myself in them, the more real I am. I am fully real if my own heart says *yes* to *everyone*.

I will be a better Catholic, not if I can *refute* every shade of Protestantism, but if I can affirm the truth in it and still go further.

So, too, with the Muslims, the Hindus, the Buddhists, etc. This does not mean syncretism, indifferentism, the vapid and careless friendliness that accepts everything by thinking of nothing. There is much that one cannot "affirm" and "accept," but first one must say "yes" where one really can.

If I affirm myself as a Catholic merely by denying all that is Muslim, Jewish, Protestant, Hindu, Buddhist, etc., in the end I will find that there is not much left for me to affirm as a Catholic: and certainly no breath of the Spirit with which to affirm it.

Conjectures of a Guilty Bystander

In the Silence of the Countryside

In my case, the word of salvation, the gospel of Jesus Christ, has led me to solitude and to silence. My vocation is rare perhaps, but contemplation does not exist only within the walls of the cloister. Every man, to live a life full of significance, is called simply to know the significant interior of life and to find ultimate significance in its proper inscrutable existence, in spite of himself, in spite of the world and appearances, in the Living God. Every man born on this earth is called to find and realize himself in Christ and, through Him, to comprehend the unity of Christ with all men, so much so that he loves them as they love themselves and is one with them almost as he is one with himself: then the spirit of Christ is one with those who love Him.

In the silence of the countryside and the forest, in the cloistered solitude of my monastery, I have discovered the whole Western Hemisphere. Here I have been able, through the grace of God, to explore the New World, without traveling from city to city, without flying over the Andes or the Amazon, stopping one day here, two there, and then continuing on. Perhaps if I had traveled in this manner, I should have seen nothing: generally those who travel most see the least.

Honorable Reader

Photograph of Thomas Merton by Sibylle Akers. Used with permission of the Merton Legacy Trust and the Thomas Merton Center at Bellarmine University.

PART 9

Work

Though Merton initially struggled to integrate his talent for writing with his call to the life of a monk, he concluded, with encouragement and guidance from his abbot, that he had to continue writing. From this experience he learned to let go of his self-projected image, concentrate on humbly accepting his life as sheer gift, and share his talent with others in the best way possible.

He also believed that we need to be willing to forgo the results of our work and learn to live without looking for immediate rewards. This is only possible through prayer, since prayer and work move in tandem. Work not informed, guided, and supported by a rich life of prayer—no matter how talented we are—is easily weakened, discouraged, and dissipated. Work without contemplation is mere activism and fosters little good. On the other hand, work connected to our inner life allows us to share in God's creative activity and provide for the needs of others.

Whether we are teachers, dancers, engineers, artists, salespeople, or mechanics, Merton invites us in this chapter to stay true to our gifts so that each of us can learn to be Christ for others. He encourages us not to give in to a frenetic work schedule, nor to blindly accept the driving competitiveness of the capitalistic marketplace. Instead, we should give time to reflection and prayer and learn to unite our will with God in the midst of our activity.

Walking with God

The life of contemplation in action and purity of heart is, then, a life of great simplicity and inner liberty. One is not seeking anything special or demanding any particular satisfaction.

One is content with what is. One does what is to be done, and the more concrete it is, the better. One is not worried about the results of what is done. One is content to have good motives and not too anxious about making mistakes. In this way one can swim with the living stream of life and remain at every moment in contact with God, in the hiddenness and ordinariness of the present moment with its obvious task.

At such times, walking down a street, sweeping a floor, washing dishes, hoeing beans, reading a book, taking a stroll in the woods—all can be enriched with contemplation and with the obscure sense of the presence of God. This contemplation is all the more pure in that one does not "look" to see if it is there. Such "walking with God" is one of the simplest and most secure ways of living a life of prayer, and one of the safest. It never attracts anybody's attention, least of all the attention of him who lives it. And he soon learns *not to want to see* anything special in himself. This is the price of liberty.

The Inner Experience

Being True to the Task

The requirements of a work to be done can be understood as the will of God. If I am supposed to hoe a garden or make a table, then I will be obeying God if I am true to the task I am performing. To do the work carefully and well, with love and respect for the nature of my task and with due attention to its purpose, is to unite myself to God's will in my work. In this way I become His instrument. He works through me. When I act as His instrument my labor cannot become an obstacle to contemplation, even though it may temporarily so occupy my mind and I cannot engage in it while I am actually doing my job. Yet my work itself will purify and pacify my mind and dispose me for contemplation.

Unnatural, frantic, anxious work, work done under pressure of greed or fear or any other inordinate passion, cannot properly speaking be dedicated to God, because God never wills such work directly. He may permit that through no fault of our own we may have to work madly and distractedly, due to our sins, and to the sins of the society in which we live. In that case we must tolerate it and make the best of what we cannot avoid. But let us not be blind to the distinction between sound, healthy work and unnatural toil.

New Seeds of Contemplation

Activity and the Inner Life

A certain depth of disciplined experience is a necessary ground for fruitful action. Without a more profound human understanding derived from exploration of the inner ground of human existence, love will tend to be superficial and deceptive. Traditionally, the ideas of prayer, meditation, and contemplation have been associated with this deepening of one's personal life and this expansion of the capacity to understand and serve others.

Contemplation in a World of Action

Contemplation and Activity

Contemplation cannot construct a new world by itself. Contemplation does not feed the hungry; it does not clothe

the naked; it does not teach the ignorant; and it does not return the sinner to peace, truth, and union with God. But without contemplation we cannot see what we do in our apostolate. Without contemplation we cannot understand the significance of the world in which we must act. Without contemplation we remain small, limited, divided, partial: we adhere to the insufficient, permanently united to our narrow group and its interests, losing sight of justice and charity, seized by the passions of the moment, and, finally, we betray Christ. Without contemplation, without the intimate, silent, secret pursuit of truth through love, our action loses itself in the world and becomes dangerous. Yet, if our contemplation is fanatic or false, our action becomes much more danger-ous. We should lose ourselves to win the world; we should humble ourselves to find Christ everywhere and to love Him in all beings.

Honorable Reader

In the Mirror of My Activity

I do not need to *see* myself, I merely need to *be* myself. I must think and act like a living being, but I must not plunge my whole self into what I think and do, or seek always to find myself in the work I have done. The soul that projects itself entirely into activity, and seeks itself outside itself in the work of its own will is like a madman who sleeps on the sidewalk in front of his house instead of living inside where it is quiet and warm. The soul that throws itself outdoors in order to find itself in the effects of its own work is like a fire that has no desire to burn but seeks only to go up in smoke.

. . . When a man constantly looks and looks at himself in the mirror of his own acts, his spiritual double vision splits him into two people. And if he strains his eyes hard enough, he forgets which one is real. In fact, reality is no longer found either in himself or in his shadow. The substance has gone out of itself into the shadow, and he has become two shadows instead of one real person.

Then the battle begins. Whereas one shadow was meant to praise the other, now one shadow accuses the other. The activity that was meant to exalt him reproaches and condemns him. It is never real enough. Never active enough. The less he is able to *be* the more he has to *do*. He becomes his own slave driver—a shadow whipping a shadow to death, because it cannot produce reality, infinitely substantial reality, out of his own nonentity.

No Man Is an Island

Seek Peace Within

All men seek peace first of all with themselves. That is necessary, because we do not naturally find rest even in our own being. . . . A man who is not at peace with himself necessarily projects his interior fighting into the society of those he lives with, and spreads a contagion of conflict all around him. Even when he tries to do good to others his efforts are hopeless, since he does not know how to do good to himself. In moments of wildest idealism he may take it into his head to make other people happy: and in doing so he will overwhelm them with his own unhappiness. He seeks to find himself somehow in the work of making others happy. Therefore he throws himself into the work. As a result he gets out of the work all that he put into it: his own confusion, his own disintegration, his own unhappiness.

It is useless to try to make peace with ourselves by being pleased with everything we have done. In order to settle down in the quiet of our own being we must learn to be detached from the results of our own activity. We must withdraw ourselves, to some extent, from effects that are beyond our control and be content with the good will and the work that are the quiet expression of our inner life.

No Man Is an Island

Manual Labor

In manual labor we become helpers and cooperators with God the creator and administrator of the world—we become instruments of his divine providence—we help Him change and renew the face of the earth. We are agents and tools of the creator Spirit. Like Adam, we are privileged to be gardeners of God's creation, and to contemplate God in and through the creatures we work with.

The Monastic Journey

Centered on Love

The essential thing in our life is this fact that it be centered on love as sufficient unto itself. Love alone is enough, regardless of whether it produces anything. It is better for love not to be especially oriented to results, to a work to be done, a class to be taught, people to be taken care of in the hospital, or anything like that. In the active life love is channeled into something that gets results. In the so-called contemplative life love is sufficient unto itself.

Contemplation in a World of Action

Working in an Agitated Way

If I work in an agitated, fearful way, I have to pay the price. There will be a result that I have to contend with. It's like saying if you go out and drink a bottle of whiskey, you're going to have a hangover the next day. That's just what happens. If you work in such a way that your work is a kind of drug, then you're going to have a hangover or a headache the next day. If your work is frenetic and demands a certain result, you may get the result. But there will be other consequences, too. You're going to suffer from doing it that way. All of us experience this. If we throw ourselves into something, looking for a special payoff for ourselves, emotional or otherwise, we know what happens. We know that it doesn't work out well. We're disappointed and frustrated. Much of this is unconscious. . . .

Sometimes we get into a kind of tantrum. Or we get into a bind. Perhaps in dealing with other people, we're too dependent on a certain kind of reaction. Like someone with musical talent who *has* to be prepared and *has* to be appreciated. In a situation like that, there's a lot of misplaced karma. Anyone who does things with a lot of concern about results, wanting praise and appreciation, will get other consequences. In this case, every time you are praised, you will need more. The principle about drugs applies to activity. Work can be a drug.

A person who wants his work to turn him on may have that happen, but then it will have to turn him on *more* the next time. He keeps finding little ways of getting satisfaction out of his work; he exploits it.

. . . If I act in a detached, free, and conscientious way, then I'm working well, I'm acting as God's instrument. Then I'm fully in accord with the great work that I don't understand, contributing my little part. The real joy and reward that's supposed to come is a constant sense that I am God's instrument and a sense of gratitude for being that. If you see work in this way, then it becomes a source of peace and a real prayer.

Seen in this light, our work is a constant adoration of God, it's constant praise of God and constant love. A person doesn't have to do any more than live and act in this ordinary way in order to be perfectly united with God.

The Springs of Contemplation

PART 10

Social Concern and the Call to Prophecy

Action for justice and peacemaking, according to Merton, are integral to a full Christian life. No one who loves Christ—whether monk or model, senator or laborer—can be exempt from putting love into action for the good of humankind.

Though the first sixteen years of monastic life removed Merton from the troubles and chaos of the world, a gradual awakening of his social consciousness began in the late 1950s and grew stronger over the next decade. Among his concerns were the nuclear devastation of Nagasaki and Hiroshima, the Cold War, and mounting racial tensions, and he became involved in the pacifist movement. His dedication to social reform evolved from his commitment to the presence of Christ in the world. Hailing the divine life that exists in everyone, Merton calls us to discover the unity that binds us all together.

However, he also understood that to grow in love and to have the strength and wisdom to challenge the fear within ourselves, as well as social ills, requires spiritual transformation. Only an inner transformation will keep us focused on God's will, God's love, and God's invitation to a full life. Love transcends individual interests. Without the deepening capacity for love that comes from inner change, we will continue to turn against one another, ignore our common ground as human beings, and fail to confront racism, violence, fear, and oppression.

In the end, Merton believed that each of us is called to be a prophet and witness to Christ in the world. He saw his life as a monk as an eschatological sign pointing to a better future and calling others to make their own hope a reality. During a time of political, social, and religious upheaval that began with World War II and included the Second Vatican Council, Merton's prophetic voice proclaimed a new day for contemporary society.

The selections in this chapter describe the parameters of Christian social action and challenge us to manifest the love of Christ by committing ourselves to the truth. We may think that it is not our job to speak out, but as Merton puts it, as contemplatives we have a responsibility to take a prophetic stance and face the road ahead. ❧

Christian Social Action

Christian social action is first of all action that discovers religion in politics, religion in work, religion in social programs for better wages, Social Security, etc., not at all to "win the worker for the Church," but because God became man, because every man is potentially Christ, because Christ is our brother, and because we have no right to let our brother live in want, or in degradation, or in any form of squalor whether physical or spiritual. In a word, if we really understood the meaning of Christianity in social life we would see it as part of the redemptive work of Christ, liberating man from misery, squalor, subhuman living conditions, economic or political slavery, ignorance, alienation.

Conjectures of a Guilty Bystander

Following Christ Perfectly

What is needed now is the Christian who manifests the truth of the Gospel in social action, with or without explanation. The more clearly his life manifests the teaching of Christ, the more salutary will it be. Clear and decisive Christian action explains itself, and teaches in a way that words never can.

What is wanted now is therefore not simply the Christian who takes an inner complacency in the words and example of Christ, but who seeks to follow Christ perfectly, not only in his own personal life, not only in prayer and penance, but also in his political commitments and in all his social responsibilities. The Christian conscience can hardly be at peace with a minimalist ethic which justifies and permits as much as possible force and terror, in international politics and in war, instead of struggling in every way to restrain force and bring into being a positive international authority which can effectively prevent war and promote peace.

Passion for Peace

A Stand for Truth

Nonviolence is perhaps the most exacting of all forms of struggle, not only because it demands first of all that one be ready to suffer evil and even face the threat of death without violent retaliation, but because it excludes mere transient self-interest from its considerations. In a very real sense, he who practices nonviolent resistance must commit himself not to the defense of his own interests or even those of a particular group: he must commit himself to the defense of objective truth and right and above all of *man*. His aim is then not simply to "prevail" or to prove that he is right and the adversary wrong, or to make the adversary give in and yield what is demanded of him.

Nor should the nonviolent resister be content to prove *to himself* that *he* is virtuous and right, and that *his* hands and heart are pure even though the adversary's may be evil and defiled. Still less should he seek for himself the psychological gratification of upsetting the adversary's conscience and perhaps driving him to an act of bad faith and refusal of the truth. We know that our unconscious motives may, at times, make our nonviolence a form of moral aggression and even a subtle provocation designed (without awareness) to bring out the evil we hope to find in the adversary, and thus to justify ourselves in our own eyes and in the eyes of "decent people." . . .

Christian nonviolence is not built on a presupposed division, but on the basic unity of man. It is not out for the conversion of the wicked to the ideas of the good, but for the healing and reconciliation of man with himself, man the person and man the human family.

Passion for Peace

The Demands of Secular Society

"Secular" society is by its nature committed to what Pascal calls "diversion," that is, to movement which has, before everything else, the anesthetic function of quieting our anguish. All society, without exception, tends to be in some respect "secular." But a genuinely secular society is one which cannot be content with innocent escapes from itself. More and more it tends to need and to demand, with insatiable dependence, satisfaction in pursuits that are unjust, evil, or even criminal. Hence the growth of economically useless businesses that exist for profit and not for real production, that create artificial needs which they then fill with cheap and quickly exhausted products. Hence the wars that arise when producers compete for markets and sources of raw material. . . . And this reminds us, of course, that the real root of secularism is godlessness.

The Inner Experience

The Root of All War

At the root of all war is fear: not so much the fear men have of one another as the fear they have of *everything*. It is not merely that they do not trust one another; they do not even trust themselves. If they are not sure when someone else may turn around and kill them, they are still less sure when they may turn around and kill themselves. They cannot trust anything, because they have ceased to believe in God.

It is not only our hatred of others that is dangerous but also and above all our hatred of ourselves: particularly that hatred of ourselves which is too deep and too powerful to be consciously faced. For it is this which makes us see our own evil in others and unable to see it in ourselves. . . .

When I pray for peace, I pray not only that the enemies of my country may cease to want war, but above all that my own country will cease to do the things that make war inevitable.

New Seeds of Contemplation

Manifesting the Love of Christ

The great historical event, the coming of the Kingdom, is made clear and is "realized" in proportion as Christians themselves live the life of the Kingdom in the circumstances of their own place and time. The saving grace of God in the Lord Jesus is proclaimed to man existentially in the love, the openness, the simplicity, the humility and the self-sacrifice of Christians. By their example of a truly Christian understanding of the world, expressed in a living and active application of the Christian faith to the human problems of their own time, Christians manifest the love of Christ for men (John 13:35, 17:21), and by that fact make him visibly present in the world. The religious basis of Christian nonviolence is then faith in Christ the Redeemer and obedience to his demand to love and manifest himself in us by a certain manner of acting in the world and in relation to other men.

. . . Furthermore, Christian nonviolence and meekness imply a particular understanding of the power of human poverty and powerlessness when they are united with the invisible strength of Christ. The beatitudes indeed convey a profound existential understanding of the dynamic of the Kingdom of God—a dynamic made clear in the parables of the mustard seed and of the yeast. This is a dynamism of patient and secret growth, in belief that out of the smallest, weakest, and most insignificant seed the greatest tree will come. This is not merely a matter of blind and arbitrary faith. The early history of the Church, the record of the apostles and martyrs remains to testify to this inherent and mysterious dynamism of the ecclesial "event" in the world of history and time. Christian nonviolence is rooted in this consciousness and this faith.

Faith and Violence

Fighting against War with Prayer and Sacrifice

Christians must become active in every possible way, mobilizing all their resources for the fight against war. First of all there is much to be studied, much to be learned. Peace is to be preached, nonviolence is to be explained as a practical method, and not left to be mocked as an outlet for crackpots who want to make a show of themselves. Prayer and sacrifice must be used as the most effective spiritual weapons in the war against war, and like all weapons they must be used with deliberate aim: not just with a vague aspiration for peace and security, but against violence and against war. This implies that we are also willing to sacrifice and restrain our own instinct for violence and aggressiveness in our relations with other people. We may never succeed in this campaign, but whether we succeed or not the duty is evident. It is the great Christian task of our time. Everything else is secondary, for the survival of the human race depends on it. We must at least face this responsibility and do something about it. And the first job of all is to understand the psychological forces at work in ourselves and in society.

Passion for Peace

A Responsibility for Creation

Perhaps the most crucial aspect of Christian obedience to God today concerns the responsibility of the Christian, in technological society, toward creation and God's will for his creation. Obedience to God's will for nature and for man; respect for nature and love for man; awareness of our power to frustrate God's designs for nature and for man, to radically corrupt and destroy natural goods by misuse and blind exploitation, especially by criminal waste.

A Vow of Conversation

My Entire Life Is a Protest

It is my intention to make my entire life a rejection of, a protest against the crimes and injustices of war and political tyranny which threaten to destroy the whole race of man and the world with him. By my monastic life and vows I am saying NO to all the concentration camps, the aerial bombardments, the staged political trials, the judicial murders, the racial injustices, the economic tyrannies, and the whole socioeconomic apparatus which seems geared for nothing but global destruction in spite of all its fair words in favor of peace. I make monastic silence a protest against the lies of politicians, propagandists, and agitators, and when I speak it is to deny that my faith and my Church can ever seriously be aligned with these forces of injustice and destruction.

. . . If I say NO to all these secular forces, I also say YES to all that is good in the world and in man. I say YES to all that is beautiful in nature, and in order that this may be the yes of a freedom and not of subjection, I must refuse to possess any thing in the world purely as my own. I say YES to all the men and women who are my brothers and sisters in the world, but for this yes to be an assent of freedom and not of subjection, I must live so that not one of them may seem to belong to me, and that I may not belong to any of them. It is because I want to be more to them than a friend that I become, to all of them, a stranger.

Honorable Reader

The World Is in Crisis

The world is in crisis. A kind of madness sweeps through human society, threatening to destroy it altogether. The faith, the love, and the patience of saints are the only forces that can save us from destruction. The Christian, in deep compassion, must seek to help his fellow man to escape from the terrible effects of greed and hatred. He must therefore be concerned with social justice and with peace on earth. It would be a grave mistake to confuse Christianity with the ideology of power and force which sometimes influences the policies of certain nations that appeal to Christianity to justify themselves.

Honorable Reader

We Are Prophetic

Any good we have is not ours; it is Christ's. Understanding this is a key point in our lives, and never forgetting it. Because the joy and consolation of our life is realizing that what we have cannot be lost, because it is God's. We can separate ourselves from it if we want to, but it is God's, and it is sure.

That is our security. Not the security of *I* am a good person, *I* am a faithful religious. It is God who is good, whose mercy is without fail. If there is fidelity in my life, thank God. God is the one who does it, in spite of me.

There's no need to worry about these things. We just let Christ be faithful to us. If we live with that kind of mind, we are prophetic. We become prophetic when we live in such a way that our life is an experience of the infallible fidelity of God. That's the kind of prophecy we are called to, not the business of being able to smell the latest fashion coming ten years before it happens. It is simply being in tune with God's mercy and will.

. . . In other words, if we trust God to act in us, God will act in us. This is how our lives become prophetic. Prophecy is not a technique, it is not about telling someone else what to do. If we are completely open to the Holy Spirit, then the Spirit will be able to lead us where God wants us to go. Going along that line, our lives will be prophetic.

The Springs of Contemplation

Be Authentic

So before we can become prophetic, we have to be authentic human beings, people who can exist outside a structure, who can create their own existence, who have within themselves the resources for affirming their identity and their freedom in any situation in which they find themselves. This means people capable of creating a life for themselves who are not identified with a structure. . . .

We're being encouraged to identify ourselves with a secular culture that in its own way offers a kind of security and comfort, but which, in fact swallows up our liberty because it's a totalitarian structure.

The Springs of Contemplation

Witnesses to the New Creation

If the contemplative is totally out of touch with the realities and the crises of his time, he loses all claim to that special fullness and maturity of wisdom which should be his. The Church has always expected that her contemplatives should be men and women who have attained a greater depth of prophetic wisdom, a more profound understanding of the Word and the love of God, so that they may be more perfect witnesses of the Kingdom and of the new creation.

Contemplation in a World of Action

A Vision of One Truth

The man who has attained final integration is no longer limited by the culture in which he has grown up. . . . He accepts not only his own community, his own society, his own friends, his own culture, but all mankind. He does not remain bound to one limited set of values in such a way that he opposes them aggressively or defensively to others. He is fully "Catholic" in the best sense of the word. He has a unified vision and experience of the one truth shining out in all its various manifestations, some clearer than others, some more definite and more certain than others. He does not set these partial views up in opposition to each other, but unifies them in a dialectic or an insight of complementarity. With this view of life he is able to bring perspective, liberty, and spontaneity, into the lives of others. The finally integrated man is a peacemaker, and that is why there is such a desperate need for our leaders to become such men of insight.

Contemplation in a World of Action

Acknowledgments

Excerpts from *The Climate of Monastic Prayer* by Thomas Merton, copyright © 1969 by the Merton Legacy Trust. Reprinted with permission of Cistercian Publications.

By Thomas Merton, from *The Collected Poems of Thomas Merton*, copyright © 1948 by New Directions Publishing Corporation, 1977 by the Trustees of the Merton Legacy Trust. Reprinted by permission of Pollinger Limited and New Directions Publishing Corp.

Excerpts from *Conjectures of a Guilty Bystander* by Thomas Merton, copyright © 1966 by the Abbey of Gethsemani, Inc. Used by permission of Doubleday, a division of Random House, Inc.

Excerpts from *Contemplation in a World of Action* by Thomas Merton, copyright © 1971 by the Trustees of the Merton Legacy Trust. Reprinted by permission of The Merton Legacy Trust.

Excerpts from *Disputed Questions* by Thomas Merton. Copyright © 1960 by the Abbey of Our Lady of Gethsemani. Copyright renewed 1988 by Alan Hanson. Reprinted by arrangement with Farrar, Straus Giroux LLC.

Excerpts from *Faith and Violence: Christian Teaching and Christian Practice* by Thomas Merton, copyright ©1968 by the